A CHRISTIAN'S JOURNEY TOWARD

SOCIAL JUSTICE, EQUALITY & FREEDOM

WASHINGTON JOHNSON II, D.MIN.

J2
PUBLISHING

CONTENTS

SEVEN REASONS NOT TO READ THIS BOOK

1 This book offers inspiring stories from Dr. Washington Johnson II's heritage as a person of faith, a theologian, chaplain, pastor, journalist, philanthropist, veteran, husband, father, son, brother, uncle, and author five generations removed from slavery.

He tackles without apology the uncomfortable truths about the economic, educational, and social impact of systemic racism, voter suppression, and social injustice in America while offering pathways of hope.

A master storyteller, the author connects the dots of his life story with American history and biblical narratives.

2 Do not read this book if you are not willing to take a prayerful stand on your knees.

President Abraham Lincoln said: "I have been driven many times upon my knees by the overwhelming conviction that I had no where else to go. My own wisdom and that of all about me seemed insufficient for that day."

This book contains illustrations of ordinary people who are so grateful and happy now that they have come boldly before God, believing and receiving extraordinary answers to their prayers.

3 Close this book if you do not believe you have the right, duty, and privilege to advocate for voting rights, justice, and a biblical framework for helping raise all people's economic, educational, and social levels within your community.

Quoting philanthropist George McLean: "It is the responsibility of the people of Mississippi to raise the level - economically, educationally, spiritually, and otherwise—of all the people of Mississippi. There is nobody else who's going to come in here and do it for us." [1]

4 Do not read this book if you do not share a life-transforming vision of social justice.

"For there is always light, if only we are brave enough to see it. If only we are brave enough to be it." National Youth Poet Laureate, Amanda Gorman. [2]

5 Do not read this book if you or your organization have no intentions of solving real-world problems. Practical steps and transformative leadership principles on the joy of developing, cultivating, and stewarding diverse, equitable, and inclusive relationships are throughout this book.

6 "E Pluribus Unum" is a wake-up call to action as God's agents of change, reconciliation, and unity. It challenges the reader to demonstrate moral courage while wrestling with the question that school principal Linda Cliatt-Wayman asks as she leads her team in fixing broken, low-performing, and persistently dangerous schools serving children in poverty. "So What, Now What, What Are We Going to Do About it?" [3]

7 Do not purchase this book if do not believe that God "Blessed You To Be A Blessing."

Proceeds from the sale of this book will benefit local charities engaging in economic, educational, spiritual, and social justice.

—Dr. Johnny Poole, Co-Founder/COO
ChaplainCare
https://chaplaincare.com

---

1. https://createfoundation.com/

2. https://www.townandcountrymag.com/society/politics/a35279603/amanda-gorman-inauguration-poem-the-hill-we-climb-transcript/

3. https://www.ted.com/talks/linda_cliatt_wayman_how_to_fix_a_broken_school_lead_fearlessly_love_hard?language=en#t-662331

DEDICATION

For my wife, Joyce, and son, Washington III;

my parents, Washington Johnson Sr. and Mildred Johnson;

my siblings, Janice, Cynthia, Stephanie, Rosalind, and Grayland.

This book is dedicated to the glory of God who makes all things possible.

I firmly believe that "I can do all things through Christ who strengthens me."
Philippians 4:13

ABOUT THE AUTHOR

Washington Johnson II, DMin was born in Birmingham, Alabama, the cradle for the American Civil Rights Movement. He is a protestant minister and advocate for social justice, who believes that social justice, equality, and freedom should be afforded to all people. His beliefs are firmly rooted in biblical principles, i.e., "Learn to do good; Seek justice, Rebuke the oppressor; Defend the fatherless, Plead for the widow." Isaiah 1:17, " "He has shown you, O man, what is good; And what does the Lord require of you But to do justly, To love mercy, And to walk humbly with your God?" Micah 6:8

His pastoral ministry spanned throughout Alabama, Tennessee, Mississippi, and Northern California, where he was actively involved in community, civic and religious affairs. He has also served as a military, campus, law enforcement, and fire department chaplain. Johnson is an alumnus of Oakwood University (Huntsville, Alabama), The Seventh-day Adventist Theological Seminary (Berrien Springs, Michigan), and Reformed Theological Seminary (Clinton, Mississippi), receiving Bachelor of Arts, Master of Divinity, and Doctor of Ministry degrees, respectively. He is married to Joyce Johnson, Ph.D., an educator, and has one son, Washington Johnson III, a medical student.

EMANCIPATION

CHAPTER 1

THE CONUNDRUM OF SLAVERY

Social justice in America is gravely lacking as a means of equality for all people, especially African Americans, and is far from God's original plan for humanity. This book presents a historical perspective of social justice, equality, and freedom in America within a biblical context since understanding the past can potentially enlighten the future.

I was reminded of this concept as I looked out the backyard window of our home on a beautiful autumn day and saw the cotton field of a farmer. I had watched the cotton develop as it was planted, irrigated, and fertilized throughout the growing process. Then the beautiful flowers bloomed, fell off, and the mature white cotton boll appeared, seemingly, overnight.

When harvested, cotton can be woven into cloth that is often used to make sheets, shirts, towels, and many other products. Although these items were not visible in the cotton field, the kaleidoscope of my imagination allowed me to see optical images of what the cotton could become in the future. Meaningful history can produce a similar effect.

My family history dates to almost one hundred and seventy-five years ago as my ancestors, who were subjects of the slave trade, arrived in America after a 90-day voyage from the continent of Africa. The slave trade was started by Portugal in the 16th century as Spain needed slave labor while the Americas were in search of gold. It grew into a profitable business as other European countries, and West African kingdoms became wealthy and powerful from the profits of the slave trade. Ironically, slavery was not a new concept since slavery in Africa had existed for hundreds of years as the result of tribal wars and the kidnapping of the vulnerable. Spreading rapidly, from 1526 to 1867, approximately "12.5 million captured men, women, and children were put on ships in Africa, and 10.7 million arrived in the Americas." https://www.gilderlehrman.org/history-resources/teacher-resources/historical-context-facts-about-slave-trade-and-slavery

1619 is often used as a reference point for teaching the origin of the institution of slavery in America, when 20 African slaves arrived in the Jamestown colony of Virginia, however, enslaved Africans had arrived long before the early 1500s. As a new nation, America struggled with the issue of slavery, which has been referred to by Senate Minority Leader Mitch McConnell (R) Kentucky and former President Barack Obama as "America's original sin." Slaves worked from sunrise to sunset in the cotton fields with the hope of experiencing freedom one day for themselves and their descendants. The cotton fields became the field of dreams as they moved from row to row with bags of cotton on their shoulders, singing "I Got Shoes:"

> *I got shoes,*
> *You got shoes,*
> *All of God's children got shoes!*
> *When I get to heaven, gonna put on my shoes;*
> *I'm gonna walk all over God's Heaven,*
> *Heaven, Heaven.*
> *Everybody talkin' 'bout Heaven ain't goin' there,*
> *Heaven, Heaven;*
> *Gonna walk all over God's Heaven!*
> —Author unknown

Despite their post-slavery optimism, African Americans experienced trauma resulting from the enactment of Jim Crow and extreme racial segregation laws. Unfortunately, the combination of slavery and these societal ills contributed to generations of traumatic experiences, or intergenerational trauma, defined by the APA (2022) as "A phenomenon in which the descendants of a person who has experienced a terrifying event show adverse emotional and behavioral reactions to the event that are similar to those of the person himself or herself." Intergenerational trauma can manifest itself in various ways, including but not limited to a heightened sense of vulnerability and helplessness, low self-esteem, depression, suicidality, substance abuse, difficulty in regulating aggression, and extreme reactivity to stress, according to the American Psychological Association (2022).

Such harmful and potentially life-threatening implications make it essential for African Americans to become aware of and seek appropriate treatment for the effects of intergenerational trauma, which could potentially affect them adversely over the course of a lifetime. However, the resilience of slaves was remarkable as they adapted and persevered, learning to sing the Lord's song in a strange land.

Throughout my own life, I have coveted the rare form of optimism exhibited by slaves as I consider my own experiences, which include many challenges, successes, and an equal number of peaks and valleys. I entered the world during the 1960s, a turbulent decade in our nation's history, with three major assignations: United States President John F. Kennedy (November 22, 1963), then Civil Rights Leader Martin Luther King Jr. (April 4, 1968); and United States Attorney General Robert Kennedy (June 6, 1968). The country also faced many global challenges during my birth era—the Cold War, the threat of a nuclear war, and the Vietnam War.

I was born in Birmingham, Alabama, on July 13, 1961, one hundred years from the American Civil War and five generations removed from slavery. My city of birth is considered the cradle of the American Civil Rights Movement. My father, Washington Johnson Sr., a World War II veteran, was employed by the United States Steel Corporation for 40 years, where his father, my grandfather, was also employed. My mother, Mildred Poole Johnson, was a nurse by profession but later served as a Bible Instructor for 42 years for the Seventh day Adventist Church. I became the fifth of six siblings, with four sisters (Janice, Cynthia, Stephanie, and Rosalind) and one brother (Grayland) following my birth two years later. My parents were people of faith who emphasized two important keys that would open doors of opportunities for the family: faith in God and achievement of higher education.

Their emphasis on these areas resulted in all six of us graduating from college, six receiving master's degrees, and two earning terminal degrees. Unfortunately, this does not align with the outlook or the norm for many African American families. We were recipients of God's amazing grace, as He inspired my parents to invest sacrificially in our future. It was not always an easy feat, as each of us attended school in the basement of our local church with multiple-grade classrooms that were taught by three teachers.

Our playground was a gravel parking lot where we regularly played kick or dodgeball when no cars were moving. We ate our brown bag lunches in the classrooms at our desks, and public transportation was our means of getting to and from school. Despite any small or big challenge, each day was filled with an abundance of learning opportunities that proved to have a life-changing effect over the years. I am certain this is due in part to the strong amplification of biblical principles that were embedded into each subject area.

I was blessed to have been born in a Christian home where moral and ethical principles were taught that helped to develop my confidence in God and provided me with an understanding of who I am in Him. In our home, we extended hospitality and financial support to strangers, family, and friends. There was even a family of nine that stayed with us for an extended period. I learned from my parents at a young age to treat others with dignity and respect. These principles are important to my own situational awareness and behavior in my personal and professional life.

During the 1950s, my parents participated in a Bible study where they learned that the seventh day of the week, Saturday, was the biblical Sabbath. This day subsequently became the day of worship for the entire family. Our worship practice was undergirded by our belief in, and literal interpretation of the fourth commandment found in Exodus 20:8-11: "Remember the Sabbath day, to keep it holy. Six days you shall labor and do all your work, but the seventh day is the Sabbath of the Lord your God. In it, you shall do no work: you, nor your son, nor your daughter, nor your male servant, nor your female servant, nor your cattle, nor your stranger who is within your gates. For in six days, the Lord made the heavens and the earth, the sea, and all that is in them, and rested the seventh day. Therefore, the Lord blessed the Sabbath day and hallowed it."

Upon becoming Sabbatarians and joining the Seventh-day Adventist Church, our worship practice involved observing the Sabbath from sunset Friday to Sunset Saturday and several dietary changes based on the scriptural writing of Leviticus 11 and Deuteronomy 14.

While delighted in the joy of our newfound faith, it also came with challenges that were mostly experienced by my father regarding his work schedule. Prior to embracing Sabbath observance, he had occasionally been assigned to weekend work. Upon becoming a Sabbatarian, he approached his supervisor and respectfully asked to have Saturdays off, offering to work any other schedule that accommodated the company. This request placed my father in a dilemma with his supervisor, who could not understand why an African American would worship on what was perceived as the Jewish Sabbath and chose to be unaccommodating. In a measured tone of voice, the supervisor informed my father that it would be impossible to avoid working on Saturday. Adding to the tensions of the time frame was the start of the American Civil Rights Movement in Birmingham, Alabama.

Ironically, Dr. Martin Luther King Jr. and other civil rights supporters were less than ten miles from my father's place of employment, advocating for desegregation that would extend some basic rights to African Americans. The intersections of race and religion comprised my father's dilemma during an era where there was no legal protection since Title VII of the Civil Rights Act of 1964, which prohibited employers from discriminating against employees or applicants for employment because of their religious beliefs, had not yet been enacted. My father had always provided for his growing family, which had increased to eight members by 1963. This was also around the time he had purchased a bigger home. Simultaneously, the employment situation was brewing and would prove to be a monumental test of his faith. His supervisor changed his work schedule weekly to force him to resign in an attempt to protect the company's interest. However, Dad (as we affectionately referred to him) was a man of great faith who had fully embraced the biblical Sabbath as a day of worship, self-care, Bible study, exploring nature with the family, and enjoying a delectable Sabbath meal. It was truly the best day of the week, which we all looked forward to. Despite what seemed to be a very bleak situation, Dad remained strong, prayerful, resilient, and true to his faith convictions. He was regularly engaged in earnest prayer with my mother, the pastor, and others, petitioning God to give his supervisor a change of heart about his work schedule. He affirmed the words of the apostles, Peter and John, in Act 5:29: "We ought to obey God rather than men," and God honored his faith by granting him a work schedule that did not require Sabbath work. Unsurprisingly, God blessed the culmination of Dad's career with United States Steel with a special award of honor and recognition—a pair of gold cuff links that continually serve as a reminder of God's faithfulness. After Dad's death in 2002, I wore the gold cuff links on special occasions. However, I have since passed them on to my son, Washington Johnson III, along with Dad's legacy of faith in a God who cares about every detail of our lives. Washington III cherishes the tangible gift as well as the faith legacy that aligns with counsel that I have shared with him on many occasions: "Challenges strengthen our faith in God and shape our characters for now and eternity. Challenges allow us to see the impossible become possible and the unimaginable become a reality. When we take inventory of the past, we will see that the providential hands of God were moving in our lives for our ultimate success, and we would not have had it any other way."

The words of Paul in Romans 8:28 are also appropriate to contemplate often during life's complexities: "And we know that all things work together for good to those who love God, to those who are the called according to His purpose."

Religious tolerance was another lesson I learned from Dad's experience. I clearly see the importance of appreciating the spiritual and religious beliefs of others without apprehension. Serving as a chaplain, I have the privilege to interact with people from various denominations and being able to effectively provide spiritual support respectively because of my early understanding of religious pluralism. Accordingly, my interest in ministry seemed to be ignited by some of the experiences of those early years. Remarkably, I sensed my call to ministry at about age six, and it was confirmed when my mother shared with me (several times) that prior to my birth, she had dedicated me to the Lord, like Hannah, the Prophet Samuel's mother "Then she made a vow and said, "O Lord of hosts, if You will indeed look on the affliction of Your maidservant and remember me, and not forget Your maidservant, but will give Your maidservant a male child, then I will give him to the Lord all the days of his life, and no razor shall come upon his head." (1 Samuel 9:11). God answered my mother's prayer by placing a desire in my heart to serve Him in ministry. Even when I may have remotely expressed interest in other careers, it was short-lived. Like the Prophet Jeremiah, "Then I said, "I will not make mention of Him, nor speak any more in His name." But His word was in my heart like a burning fire shut up in my bones; I was weary of holding it back, And I could not." (Jeremiah 20:9).

My mother (affectionately referred to as "Mom") often shared that "lost time can never be regained," and putting things off only increases stress and anxiety. Personal journaling has been a helpful strategy for identifying opportunities for continuous improvement, allowing me to reflect on what I can do better as soon as the next day.

Mom encouraged all her children to succeed and made it known in no uncertain terms. However, her emphasis was always on achievements that would have eternal value. A retired minister shared a story with me about Mom that illustrates this point quite well. As a religious educator, conducting Bible studies was a regular part of her work. During the peak of the Civil Rights Movement in the 1960s, Mom joined others as an advocate for justice and fairness, always ready to take a stand for what was right. However, she was passionate about sharing the good news of salvation and did it with high energy.

On one occasion, she had given a series of Bible studies to a young lady (whom we'll pseudo-name Onia) who decided to be baptized at the end of the study series. However, on the day the baptism was scheduled, Mom learned that Onia would not be present for her baptism because a peace march was scheduled in which she planned to participate. Though fully committed to the cause that prompted the march, Mom knew that Onia's salvation was more important and would favorably impact every part of her life. Consequently, she was inspired to drive to where the march was being carried out. She arrived while the marchers were assembling and went through the crowd, asking other marchers if they knew Onia.

Finally, Mom caught a glimpse of Onia, immediately approached her, and lovingly said, "your baptismal robe is waiting at the church." Onia was so impressed by Mom's personal interest in her eternal well-being that she immediately agreed to go to the church and be baptized. However, she first wanted to let her friends know that she would not participate in the march as planned. Mom responded with the story of the young man in the parable in Luke 9:61 who wanted to follow Jesus but first requested to tell his family: "Lord, I will follow You, but let me first go and bid them farewell who are at my house." Jesus knew that the young man's family would discourage him, and he would miss out on being a disciple of Jesus and, potentially, eternal life. Similarly, Mom affirmed Onia for her courageous stance on social justice issues but stressed that where she would spend eternity was more important. Onia was baptized that day and later shared with Mom, "Thank you for encouraging my baptism. My life is forever changed for the better." Clearly, Mom's actions reflected her hope for a better day, where there would be lasting peace, joy, and happiness. At ninety-two (at the time of this publication), she continues to prioritize the good news of the gospel while simultaneously advocating for social justice, equality, and freedom by boldly speaking out for these basic rights within her sphere.

The nurturing of my parents, my relationship with Jesus Christ, and my own lived experience as an African American have shaped my worldview, which is primarily based on biblical principles. Based on the writings of the Bible, I am completely confident of the existence of a God who is—omnipotent, omniscient, omnipresent, compassionate, and caring. He is the God of heaven and earth who created the world and mankind in His image. Therefore, all people, regardless of ethnicity, culture, gender, social or economic status, have intrinsic value in the eyesight of God.

Inspired by a heartfelt desire to see positive change on many fronts in America, this book explores the history and conundrum of slavery, the continual disparate treatment of African Americans, and action-oriented solutions. It is my hope that readers will gain insight and increased awareness that will open the windows of understanding on this important topic that will prompt positive change in society and within the hearts of humanity.

SLAVERY, COMPROMISES AND BROKEN PROMISES

Thomas Jefferson and other prominent signers of the Declaration of Independence owned slaves and knew that the issue of slavery could possibly divide the nation. During the 1787 Constitutional Convention, a three-fifths compromise was agreed upon between delegates from the North and the South. It granted "Slaveholding states the right to count three-fifths of their slave population when it came to apportioning the number of a state's representatives to Congress."[1]

However, tension and partisan politics continued to grow over slavery. "Between 1774 and 1804, most of the northern states abolished slavery."[2] Southern states made no apologies for slavery and continued to import slaves until The United States Congress voted to ban slave importation on March 2, 1807. Later, slave trading became a capital offense in 1820. According to Eric Foner, DeWitt Clinton Professor Emeritus of History at Columbia University, "The Ban was not totally enforced, but it certainly ended what had been before then an open, legal and fairly large slave trade." https://www.npr.org/templates/story/story.php?storyId=17988106 This was a setback to the economy in the South and created resentment and distrust of the federal government.

The South needed slaves to harvest their cash crops such as cotton, rice, tobacco, and sugarcane. Hiring indentured servants was not perceived as a profitable option because they were entitled to certain rights which included, but was not limited to housing, clothing, and food. Slaves could be bought and sold, but indentured servants were not considered property and were free upon the end of their contract for a period of four or seven years. They had limited access to the court system and could own land and legally marry and have families without the fear of being sold or separated.

On the other hand, owning slaves was a profitable business. Jason Kottke offered a concise description of slave profitability: "Because slaves were property, Southern slave owners could mortgage them to banks and then the banks could package the mortgages into bonds and sell the bonds to anyone anywhere in the world, even where slavery was illegal." https://kottke.org/16/02/a-history-of-the-slave-breeding-industry-in-the-united-states In 1860 Timothy Meaher "Wagered another wealthy white man that he could bring a cargo of enslaved Africans aboard a ship into Mobile despite the 1807 Act Prohibiting the Importation of Slaves." https://nmaahc.si.edu/explore/initiatives/slave-

1 https://www.britannica.com/topic/The-Founding-Fathers-and-Slavery-1269536
2 https://www.history.com/topics/black-history/slavery

wrecks-project/africatown-alabama-usa

Meaher hired Captain William Foster to travel to the Kingdom of Dahomey (present-day Benin), using a two-masted wooden schooner named Clotilda which measured " 86 feet long and 23 feet wide." https://www.pbs.org/newshour/show/how-discovery-of-the-slave-ship-clotilda-informs-u-s-history Captain Foster purchased 110 slaves at $100.00 each who were prisoners of tribal warfare. After a 120-day voyage, the schooner arrived in the Mobile Bay and was destroyed by fire shortly after to remove all evidence of the illegal slave trade.

However, on May 22, 2019, the Clotilda was discovered in the muddy waters of the Mobile Bay, representing the last documented slave ship from Africa to reach the United States. After the end of the Civil War, they unsuccessfully attempted to raise funds to return to Africa. However, they later purchased land from the Meaher family and " Formed a society rooted in their beloved homeland, complete with a chief, a system of laws, churches and a school." https://www.smithsonianmag.com/smithsonian-institution/clotilda-last-known-slave-ship-arrive-us-found-180972177/ The community they established is called Africatown which is located approximately three miles north of downtown Mobile, AL. As of this writing plans for revitalization of Africatown are underway, including a welcome center that will tell the story of this historic site.

In 1803, America experienced expansion, nearly doubling in size, because of the "Louisiana Purchase" from the French First Republic. Missouri, which was a part of the Louisiana Purchase, petitioned to be admitted to the Union as a slave state. During this period, there were 11 free states in the North and 11 slave states in the South. Missouri's admission to the Union would tip the balance of power in the United States Congress in favor of Southern politicians who wanted to expand slavery. Therefore, the best option to keep the Union united was the Missouri Compromise of 1820, which would accept Missouri as a slave state and admit Maine, which at the time was part of Massachusetts, as a free state. The Missouri Comprise of 1820 "Banned slavery from the remaining Louisiana Purchase lands located north of the 36°30' N parallel (the southern border of Missouri)." [3]

For a time, the Missouri Compromise of 1820 kept the Union together, which was on the verge of splitting over slavery. About thirty years later, The Compromise of 1850 admitted California as a free state, left Utah and New Mexico to decide for themselves, and defined a new Texas-New Mexico bound-

---

[3] https://www.history.com/topics/abolitionist-movement/missouri-compromise

ary. However, to appease the South, the United States Congress passed The Fugitive Slave Act, which required citizens to return runway slaves to their owners. Many abolitionists felt it was tantamount to kidnapping and spoke in strong opposition to the law.

Each compromise was intended to prevent a civil war, but the Kansas-Nebraska Act, signed into law on May 30, 1854, brought the nation closer to war than ever. It repealed the Missouri Compromise of 1820, creating two new territories from land purchased earlier from the Louisiana Purchase. Unsurprisingly, "anti-slavery supporters were outraged because, under the terms of the Missouri Compromise of 1820, slavery would have been outlawed in both territories since they were both north of the 36°30' N dividing line between "slave" and "free" states."[4]

Pro-slavery supporters embraced the popular sovereignty doctrine that "People of federal territories should decide for themselves whether their territories would enter the Union as free or slave states."[5] This contention resulting from the opposing views led to physical altercations between both sides, and historians believe "55 people were killed between 1855 and 1859."[6] The ongoing fighting was referred to as Bleeding Kansas because of the bloodshed during this period.

The abolitionist John Brown, who was responsible for raids in Kansas and later captured at Harper's Ferry and sentenced to death, had prophesied the nation's fate earlier. The compromises had failed, and the stage was set for what the nation feared. John Brown's prophetic words before his execution would come true: "I, John Brown, am now quite certain that the crimes of this guilty land will never be purged away, but with Blood. I had vainly flattered myself that without very much bloodshed, it might be done."[7]

Despite the profound words in the Declaration of Independence, "All men are created equal," eighty-five years later, on April 12, 1861, the nation was battling against itself, in the American Civil War, over slavery—the deadliest war in the nation's history, with about 620,000 dead. And though the slaves were now free, the end of the war came with the broken promise of 40 acres of land and a

---

4 https://www.archives.gov/milestone-documents/kansas-nebraska-act

5 https://www.britannica.com/topic/popular-sovereignty

6 https://www.history.com/topics/19th-century/bleeding-kansas

7 https://www.pbs.org/wgbh/americanexperience/features/brown-hanging/#:~:text=When%20Brown%20emerged%20from%20his,purged%20away%2C%20but%20with%20Blood.

mule—a pseudo-freedom, at best, for America's Black population.

Following the end of the war, on April 9, 1865, Southern states immediately passed laws, i.e., Black Codes, that, in essence, perpetuated the system of slavery by restricting freedoms and forcing African Americans to work for low wages. During this period, former slaves also faced increased lynching, voter suppression, and denial of education. Fast forward to the 1960s, some of the same hurdles that crippled progress among enslaved African Americans continued to plague the nation: Jim Crow Laws enforced local and state segregation, resulting in African Americans experiencing substandard living, mortgage loan inequities, unequal pay, and disproportionate healthcare coverage.

By this time, African Americans, such as my grandfather, father, and three uncles, had served bravely in the armed forces, although in segregated units. Yet, over the following decades, they faced ongoing discrimination and segregation: in school systems, public transportation, restrooms, drinking fountains, and many other commercial establishments. Segregation seemed sewn into the fabric of America, like baseball and apple pie. Some elected officials worked feverishly to maintain the notion of "separate but equal" by perpetuating these ideologies. Governor George C. Wallace of Alabama, who, in his 1963 inaugural address, touted "Segregation now, Segregation Forever" to an enthusiastic and arousing crowd, is just one example.

Similar issues are evident today. While researchers were seeking a vaccine for the COVID-19 virus, our nation reacted to the senseless and unnecessary death of George Floyd on May 25, 2020, in Minneapolis. As Mr. Floyd was gasping for breath, police officer Derek Chauvin's knee was on his neck. During the 9 minutes and 29-second ordeal, Mr. Floyd said, "I can't breathe," while three other police officers watched without intervening.

The Minneapolis Police Department initially released a statement describing the arrest as: "Man dies after medical incident during police interaction."[8] However, Darnella Frazier, 17, recorded the incident and uploaded it on social media. Floyd's death ignited protests globally against police brutality, especially towards African Americans. Chauvin was arrested and later released on conditional bail after posting a bond of one million dollars. During the trial, Frazier testified that she had spent nights apologizing to Floyd, though he was deceased, for "not doing more."

On April 20, 2021, after three weeks of testimony, a jury of six whites and

8 https://www.boston.com/news/national-news/2021/04/23/initial-police-release-george-floyd

six people of color found Chauvin guilty on three counts: unintentional second-degree murder, third-degree murder, and second-degree manslaughter. The verdict brought a sense of closure to the Floyd family and others who watched, even at the White House. While justice for African Americans has been slow, sometimes advancing at a snail's pace, jurors appeared to be at their best in this case. On June 25, 2021, Chauvin was sentenced to twenty-two, and a half years in prison, although the sentence fell short of the thirty years, prosecutors had requested.

Sadly, there are other incidents of this magnitude, as well as a growing list of African Americans whose lives have ended by law enforcement officers: including Daunte Demetrius Wright, Breonna Taylor, and ironically, Eric Garner, who uttered the exact words as George Floyd, "I can't breathe," proving also to be some of his last words.

THE TULSA, OKLAHOMA MASSACRE

The Tulsa race riot and massacre of 1921 and mass shootings in Charleston, South Carolina (2015) and Buffalo, New York (2022) are among more examples of extreme racism that resulted in the loss of many precious lives. The Tulsa race massacre took place on May 31 through June 1, 1921, when white residents were deputized with weapons by the city police department when the "Tulsa Tribune reported that a black man, Dick Rowland, attempted to rape a white woman, Sarah Page."[9]

Rowland worked as a shoe shiner and needed to take the elevator to the segregated restroom. On entering the elevator, he accidentally tripped, catching her arm and causing Sarah to scream. The clerk on the first floor reported the incident as a sexual assault. Some whites refused to wait for an investigation as the nineteen-year-old Rowland was in custody. Page, the seventeen-year-old elevator operator, "Never filed any charges against Mr. Rowland, and she denied the claims made by the Tulsa Tribune that her clothes were torn and she was scratched during the encounter."[10]

Within a short while, it was rumored that Rowland would be lynched, and African Americans World War I Veterans arrived at the courthouse to protect Rowland. These decorated veterans were perceived as a threat to the city officials.

---

9 https://daily.jstor.org/the-devastation-of-black-wall-street/

10 https://theblackwallsttimes.com/2021/08/13/the-real-sarah-page-center-for-public-secrets-reveals-full-identity-of-woman-whose-false-allegation-launched-tulsa-race-massacre/#:~:text=Rowland%20became%20a%20wanted%20man,the%20truth%20didn't%20matter.

The veterans were from the Greenwood District, a thriving community with African American professionals, entrepreneurs, a business district, a hospital, a school system, and churches. Booker T. Washington coined it as the Black Wall Street because it had the wealthiest population of African Americans in the nation, with a dollar exchanging hands several times before leaving the community. However, this economic powerhouse was envied by the greater Tulsa area because of the prosperity of African Americans.

Without warning, the Greenwood district was attacked as buildings, homes, schools, and churches were burned and destroyed, covering more than 35 square blocks. Over 800 people were injured, and "Historians now believe as many as 300 people may have died."[11]

The insurance companies refused to pay all except one of the claims of African Americans whose property losses were more than significant, estimated at 27 million in today's dollars.[12] Ultimately, the Tulsa Tribune incited a riot that led to one of the most horrific acts of domestic terrorism against African Americans in this nation's history.

CHARLESTON, SOUTH CAROLINA CHURCH SHOOTING

The shooting at the Emanuel African Methodist Episcopal Church, on June 17, 2015, in Charleston, South Carolina, touched a sensitive cord in the nation's history when Pastor Clementa C. Pinckney, who also served as a member of the South Carolina State Senate, along with nine of his members were mercilessly killed during a weekly Bible study.

The shooter was Dylann Roof, a twenty-one-year-old male from Shelby, North Carolina, who said his intention was "to agitate race relations."[13] The members had warmly welcomed Roof as he asked to sit next to the pastor and participated in the Bible study. He later started to disagree with some of the discussion, causing confusion. As the members started to pray, he said African Americans were "taking over the country"[14] and opened fire. During the rampage, he said, "Y'all want something to pray about; I'll give you something to pray about."[15] He later attempted to take his own life, according to a survivor.

---

11 https://www.tulsahistory.org/exhibit/1921-tulsa-race-massacre/

12 https://www.brookings.edu/research/the-true-costs-of-the-tulsa-race-massacre-100-years-later/

13 https://www.cnn.com/2016/12/09/us/dylann-roof-trial-charleston-video/index.html

14 https://www.history.com/this-day-in-history/charleston-ame-church-shooting

15 https://www.washingtonpost.com/news/post-nation/wp/2015/06/20/what-we-know-so-far-about-charleston-church-shooting-suspect-dylann-roof/

President Barack Obama delivered the eulogy for the Emanuel Church victims and said, "As a nation, out of this terrible tragedy, God has visited grace upon us, for he has allowed us to see where we've been blind."[16]

We must open our eyes and address the issue of racism through dialogue, education, and achieving steps that will bring healing. Roof was sentenced to death on January 10, 2017, and to life in prison without parole on April 10, 2017. During his trial, he expressed no remorse for his actions. "I would like to make it crystal clear. I do not regret what I did," Roof wrote. "I am not sorry."[17]

Members of the victims' families expressed their faith in God and forgiveness of Roof, which was a necessary step towards healing, but not an excuse for his actions.

BUFFALO, NEW YORK SUPERMARKET SHOOTING

On May 14, 2022, Payton Gendron, an eighteen-year-old male, traveled approximately 200 miles from Conklin, New York, to Buffalo, New York, where he targeted the Tops Friendly supermarket. Heavily armed and wearing military gear, Gendron killed ten people, gripping the nation. It was later discovered that Gendron "wrote that online research led him to target the 14208 zip code because it has a higher Black population than other locations he was considering."[18]

He had planned on attacking a church and elementary school before deciding on a supermarket. Following the shooting, he exited the store, then surrendered to law enforcement, and was taken into custody.

President Joseph Biden and first lady Jill Biden visited Buffalo two days later. President Biden offered prayers for the victims and their families and said, "In America, evil will not win, I promise you. Hate will not prevail."[19]

Gendron was arraigned in Erie County Court on June 2, 2022, and pled not guilty to all 25 charges. The United States Department of Justice investigated the shooting in Buffalo "as a hate crime."[20]

---

16 https://obamawhitehouse.archives.gov/the-press-office/2015/06/26/remarks-president-eulogy-honorable-reverend-clementa-pinckney

17 https://atlantablackstar.com/2017/01/04/dylann-roof-like-make-crystal-clear-dont-regret/

18 https://www.cnn.com/2022/06/02/us/buffalo-mass-shooting-suspect-indictment/index.html

19 https://www.npr.org/2022/05/18/1099680636/biden-calls-for-unity-during-his-visit-to-buffalo-which-is-shaken-by-mass-shooti

20 https://www.justice.gov/opa/pr/justice-department-statement-mass-shooting-buffalo-ny

On February 15, 2023 after listening to heartfelt statements from the families of the victims, Payton was sentenced in court to life in prison without the possibility of parole by Erie County Court Judge Susan Eagan. She said "The damage you have caused is too great and the people you have hurt are too valuable to this community." https://www.washingtonpost.com/national-security/2023/02/15/buffalo-shooting-gendron-sentencing/ Payton said in a brief statement of apology "I did a terrible thing that day. I shot and killed people because they were Black. Looking back now, I can't believe I actually did it. I believed what I read online and acted out of hate." https://www.cnn.com/2023/02/15/us/buffalo-tops-grocery-shooting-payton-gendron-state-sentencing/index.html

There is a need for more accountability from social media giants that allow hate groups to recruit, solicit funds, distribute their message online and incite people to hate. Perpetrators often search the internet for like-minded online communities which can have serious consequences and often precedes acts of violence. It worth noting that there has been a decline in hate groups, why? "Extremist groups are declining because the ideas that mobilize now operate so openly in the political mainstream." https://abc11.com/southern-poverty-law-center-hate-groups-extremist-left-wing/11636638/

However, "Many hate groups have moved to social media platforms and use of encrypted apps, while others have been banned altogether from mainstream social media networks." https://www.csmonitor.com/USA/2021/0201/Report-Some-hate-groups-disband-others-move-to-online-networks However, "Even since these bans and policy changes, some extremism on mainstream social media remains undetected, particularly in private Facebook Groups and on private Twitter accounts." https://www.vox.com/recode/22913046/deplatforming-extremists-ban-qanon-proud-boys-boogaloo-oathkeepers-three-percenters-trump

It is imperative to take action to end online hate through establishing regulations for social media companies, ensuring that there is protections against online hate and harassment. The United States Congress and the Department of Justice must continue to collaborate to enact legislation that will prevent online hate groups and the Department of Justice must convict and prosecute extreme racist group using the social media platform to spread hate.

African Americans are still the largest bias incident victim ethnic group, according to the United States Department of Justice 2020 Federal Bureau of

Investigation Federal hate crimes statistics.[21]

BLACK LIVES MATTER

The Black Lives Matter (BLM) movement is an international organization founded by "Three female Black organizers — Alicia Garza, Patrisse Cullors, and Opal Tometi."[22]

The objective of BLM is to "Highlight racism, discrimination, and inequality experienced by black people."[23] BLM started with a social media hashtag, #BlackLivesMatter, after the acquittal of George Zimmerman, a neighborhood watch volunteer in Sanford, FL, who fatally shot Trayvon Martin, an unarmed 17 year old African American male who was visiting his relatives in a gated community when he encountered an altercation with Zimmerman. BLM also gained national headlines globally during the George Floyd protests in the United States in 2020. Research conducted by the Crowd Sourcing Consortium estimated "15 million - 26 million" participated in the protests.[24]

All lives are important in the sight of God; however, African American lives are at a higher risk, in some cases, due to excessive force by law enforcement officers. President Barack Obama, during his administration, attempted to explain the difference between Black Lives Matter and All Lives Matter. He said, "I think that the reason that the organizers used the phrase Black Lives Matter was not that they were suggesting that no one else's lives matter... rather what they were suggesting was there is a specific problem that is happening in the African American community that's not happening in other communities."[25]

BLM has faced criticism, referred to as a Marxist group, which is openly seeking to overturn society and promote anti-law enforcement. There are also organizations that were formed to counter BLM, such as Blue Lives Matter, in support of law enforcement. While I strongly support law enforcement officers and greatly appreciate their service, policemen can change their uniforms when they are not on duty, but that is not as simple of a solution for African Americans who would have to change their skin color in order to avoid racial discrimination.

In an interview with ABC news, Harry Dunn, a United States Capitol

21 https://www.justice.gov/crs/highlights/2020-hate-crimes-statistics

22 https://library.law.howard.edu/civilrightshistory/BLM

23 https://www.bbc.com/news/explainers-53337780

24 https://carrcenter.hks.harvard.edu/news/black-lives-matter-may-be-largest-movement-us-history

25 https://www.pbs.org/newshour/politics/obama-defends-black-lives-matter-movement

police officer, shared a chilling story while on duty during the January 6 insurrection. He was beaten with a Blue Lives Matter flag and then responded, "Is this America? They beat police officers with Blue Lives Matter flags."[26] During the BLM protest in the nation's capital after the death of George Floyd, former President Donald Trump asked former Defense Sectary Mark Esper, "Can't you just shoot them? Just shoot them in the legs or something?[27]

There are many questions and concerns regarding BLM. However, this movement has raised awareness and subliminally articulated a message that, if properly carried out in peaceful protests, the likelihood increases for healing in a society that is challenged by a long history of injustice and inequality among persons of color. In Genesis 2:7, God breathed His breath into man's nostrils at creation. So, what right does anyone have to take God's breath from another, let alone through inhumane and violent means?

WAKE UP, WORLD!

"Wake Up Everybody" was the title of an album released by Harold Melvin & the Blue Notes in 1975 that featured the name of the album's hit song. The lyrics offer the semblance of a prophetic voice in the wildness, calling doctors, teachers, builders, politicians, and preachers to make the world a better place to live.

The lyrics were most fitting during the 70s as the United States experienced war in Southeast Asia (Vietnam), the resignation of President Richard Nixon, record unemployment, drug addiction, a gas shortage, and racial tensions that have transcended subsequent decades.

Those lyrics call us to wake up and change our way of thinking. But further, they encourage us to teach the next generation and educate the young to break the cycle. I encourage you to locate this song and listen to it—but more, to heed its message. It leans on a protest theme: wake up!

George Floyd's death was a wake-up call for America and many parts of the world, prompting thousands to protest both the present and past horrors of injustice and oppression. While such societal ills have helped to shape the present ideologies, these ills must not be allowed to continue. Changing backward thinking of injustice and oppression requires being intentional and purposeful

---

26 https://www.thedenverchannel.com/news/national/capitol-officer-they-beat-law-enforcement-with-blue-lives-matter-flags

27 https://www.8newsnow.com/news/esper-trump-asked-about-shooting-protesters-in-the-legs-or-something-after-george-floyd-death/

about creating an environment where the playing field is level. Now is the time for everyone to stand united on principle, acknowledging that history will serve as a judge of our present actions by our children and grandchildren.

The time has come for men and women of every ethnicity to be true to themselves and to speak truth to power by compelling legislative justice for all people. They must be the voice for those without a voice, a shield for the oppressed and marginalized. In his letter from the Birmingham Jail, Dr. Martin Luther King Jr. said: "Injustice anywhere is a threat to justice everywhere. We are caught in an inescapable network of mutuality, tied in a single garment of destiny. Whatever affects one directly affects all indirectly." What a relevant description of the implications of the present-day turmoil in the United States of America.

WHAT SHALL WE DO?

We must begin by taking a stand on our knees. It's called prayer, and it is a mighty difference-maker that can move mountains, tear down walls, and build bridges of hope. Regardless of how chaotic things appear, God is still in control and hears the sincere prayers of His children. True to the words of the Negro Spiritual, "He's Got the Whole World in His Hands," and the national motto of the United States, "In God We Trust." Both individual and united prayers are necessary to effect the positive change needed in our hearts, homes, this nation, and the world.

We must demonstrate compassion to all humanity as embodied in the two greatest commandments: "You shall love the LORD your God with all your heart, with all your soul, and with all your mind." This is the first and great commandment. And the second is like it: "You shall love your neighbor as yourself." (Matthew 22:37-39) Such love promotes the abandonment of every semblance of prejudice against those of a different race. For there is no room for racial intolerance in the multiethnic family of God: "There is neither Jew nor Greek, there is neither slave nor free, there is neither male nor female; for you are all one in Christ Jesus." (Galatians 3:28)

We must exercise the right to vote as a civic duty. African Americans, in particular, must actively acknowledge the importance of the Voting Rights Act of 1965, which dismantled many barriers that prevented them from exercising voting rights, as guaranteed under the 15th Amendment to the United States Constitution.

We must be agents of change. Institutional and cultural change starts with building strong, sustainable relationships with key stakeholders before crises, i.e., police departments and state and local government officials. Mahatma Gandhi's admonition states it correctly: "Be the change that you wish to see in the world." Without change, we become complacent and stagnant. On the other hand, agents of change can be catalysts for creating something new and better. The Greatest Change Agent and Master Teacher said in John 13:15a-17;

"I have set you an example that you should do as I have done for you. I tell you the truth, no servant is greater than his master, nor is a messenger greater than the one who sent him. Now that you know these things, you will be blessed if you do them."

We must seek unity within our nation by setting aside political and other differences that promote division. On the Great Seal of the United States of America are the words "E Pluribus Unum," Latin for "One out of many" or "One from many." If we do not work together to unify the races, we will experience the full impact of Jesus' statement in Mark 3:25, "And if a house be divided against itself, that house cannot stand."

On June 16, 1858, more than 1,000 delegates met in the Springfield, Illinois, statehouse for the Republican State Convention. At 5:00 p.m., they chose Abraham Lincoln as their candidate for the U.S. Senate, running against Democrat Stephen A. Douglas. At 8:00 p.m., Lincoln delivered this address to his Republican colleagues in the Hall of Representatives. The title reflects part of the speech's introduction, "A House Divided Against Itself Cannot Stand," a concept familiar to Lincoln's audience as a statement by Jesus recorded in all three synoptic gospels (Matthew, Mark, Luke).

Even Lincoln's friends regarded the speech as too radical for the occasion. His law partner, "William H. Herndon, considered Lincoln morally courageous but politically incorrect."[28]

God is calling us to demonstrate radical moral courage. Like Jesus and United States President Abraham Lincoln, we must dialogue, publicly and privately, to better understand the pain, hurt, and fear of the reoccurring plague of injustice in America.

Through the power of God, we must commit ourselves to live, love, and work together as we prepare to enter God's glorious and emerging kingdom. For the Bible tells us in Revelation 7:9 that we will all stand together before

---

[28] http://www.abrahamlincolnonline.org/lincoln/speeches/house.htm

the throne and before the Lamb: "After these things I looked, and behold, a great multitude which no one could number, of all nations, tribes, peoples, and tongues, standing before the throne and before the Lamb, clothed with white robes, with palm branches in their hand."

At last, the incredible promise proclaimed by the prophetic voice of the lyrical poet, Isaiah, will be fulfilled: "He shall judge between the nations, and rebuke many people; They shall beat their swords into plowshares, and their spears into pruning hooks; Nation shall not lift sword against nation, Neither shall they learn war anymore." (Isaiah 2:4).

This book will promote elements of social justice, equality, and freedom that must exist for all to thrive in America.

REFLECTING MORE ON THE TOPIC:

What were your most meaningful takeaways from this chapter?

____

____

____

____

What will you do differently because of your increased awareness?

____

____

____

____

What resources or support do you need to ensure the successful achievement of your goals?

____

____

____

____

WELCOME TO
AM PAR

CHAPTER 2

TAKING A STAND ON OUR KNEES

"Taking a Knee" is what the professional sports leagues call it when players kneel rather than stand for a cause during the National Anthem. Symbolically and in a spiritual sense, taking a stand on one's knees is called prayer. Prayer moves mountains, tears down walls, and builds bridges of hope. Prayer allows petitioners to talk with God, who has "got the whole world in His hands."

As the nation navigates through uncharted waters and times of uncertainty, wisdom and keen discernment will be required to address the systemic and manifold injustices that continually impede progress and unity. The source of these essential elements is of a divine nature and can only be acquired through prevailing prayer that is cyclonic and earth-shaking.

In the Torah, it is recorded that fragrant fumes ascended from the Altar of Incense as the priests burned the morning and evening sacrifices which represented the prevailing prayers of God's people. As the cloud of incense ascended, the divine glory of God descended. Once a year, on the Day of Atonement, Yom Kippur, the high priest entered the Holy of Holies with incense and burning coals from the altar of burnt offerings. The high priest was the mediator between God and the people and was the only one who performed this ecclesiastical duty. This ancient and sacred ceremony reminds us of the current intercessory work of Christ, our High Priest, in the heavenly sanctuary "Seeing then that we have a great High Priest who has passed through the heavens, Jesus the Son of God…" (Hebrews 4:14).

As the ancient altar of incense represented the prayers of God's people coming up before Him continually, our prayers today must prevail until the answer comes.

Prayer is a heaven-ordained means of making appeals, petitions, and entreaties between God and humankind "For there is one God and one Mediator between God and men, the Man Christ Jesus." (1 Timothy 2:5).

David petitioned the Lord: "Let my prayer be set before You as incense, The lifting up of my hands as the evening sacrifice." (Psalm 141:2). Zacharias was performing his priestly duty when he entered the temple to burn incense. "According to the custom of the priesthood, his lot fell to burn incense when he went into the temple of the Lord. And the whole multitude of the people was praying outside at the hour of incense." (Luke 1:9-10). Incense in Revelation represents the fervent prayers of the saints "Now when He had taken the scroll, the four living creatures and the twenty-four elders fell down before the Lamb, each having a harp, and golden bowls full of incense, which are the prayers of the saints." (Revelation 5:8).

SOLOMON'S PRAYER

In 2 Chronicles 7, Solomon's prayer at the temple's dedication in Jerusalem affirmed God's love for His chosen people, whom He had delivered from Egypt and led into the Promised Land. He expected them to obey His Commandments given at Mt. Sinai and not to become mesmerized by the idolatry of the neighboring nations. God's appeal to Solomon was: "If My people who are called by My name will humble themselves, and pray and seek My face, and turn from their wicked ways, then I will hear from heaven, and will forgive their sin and heal their land." (2 Chronicles 7:14).

This ageless appeal is most fitting for our nation today, especially during some of its challenging times, such as the pandemic. God wants to make good on His promise that if we call His name, He will "heal our land." Though prayer is critical in addressing our nation's stark injustices and moral decline, it is greatly lacking. It seems that America, the greatest and most blessed nation on earth, has forgotten God, as evidenced by, among other things, wealth disparity, social injustices, and the neglect of His Commandments. Yet God seems to be holding out the olive branch of peace, repentance, reconciliation, and restoration for those who will come boldly before His throne of grace in earnest and fervent prayer. He is waiting to do what He has done throughout biblical history through miraculously answered prayers.

Moses prayed for Israel in the wilderness, pleading with God to preserve His name and character and not destroy Israel and God answered. (Exodus 32:9-14).

Abraham prayed for Sodom, interceding for the salvation of his nephew and his family, and God answered. (Genesis 18:16-33).

Hannah Prayed for a Son who became a priest, Prophet and judge for the people of God during a crucial period in their history. (1 Samuel 1: 9-28).

David Prayed for pardon and confession of sin and was referred to as a man after God's own heart. (Psalm 51).

Elisha Prayed for his Servant's Eyes to open, and the servant saw the army of God with chariots of fire and horses. (2 Kings 6:15-17).

Hezekiah prayed for deliverance and healing, and God answered with an amazing recovery and an additional fifteen years. (2 Kings 19:14-19; 20:1-7).

Daniel's prayer of confession on behalf of God's disobedient people resulted in God answering with deliverance and restoration. (Daniel 9:1-19).

Nehemiah prayed for success. God answered with permission to rebuild the walls of Jerusalem and all the resources for the project. (Nehemiah 1:1-9, 2:1-8).

The classic "Lord's Prayer" taught by Jesus to His disciples and given as a pattern for our prayers is still answered daily. (Matthew 6:9-13).

Jesus' Prayer of Submission at Gethsemane. Beneath the shadow of the cross, Jesus petitions His Father to remove the cup of crucifixion. Then ultimately, for His Father's will to be done at Calvary for all who will personally accept Him as Lord and Savior. (Luke 22:39-46).

There is no shortage of evidence that prayer works like breath—without which we cannot live.

THREE MINISTERS KNEELING

The Kelly Ingram Park, located in Birmingham, Alabama, was the central gathering ground for peaceful protests during the American Civil Rights movement of the 1960s. It was at this park on May 3, 1963, that public safety commissioner Eugene "Bull" Connor authorized law enforcement officers, K-9s, and men with firehoses to arrest those protesting for the desegregation of public facilities in Birmingham.

Malicious attacks on children and students in their peaceful demonstrations went viral in the news. Sculptures stand in the park today depicting the tragedy where civil rights marchers were assaulted with canines and water cannons. The events in Kelly Ingram Park—and later the March on Washington in 1963, where Dr. Martin Luther King Jr delivered his famous "I Have a Dream" speech at the Lincoln memorial—became the prototypes for nonviolent and peaceful protests of the American Civil Rights movement.

The Kelly Ingram Park is located just across the street from the Sixteenth Street Baptist Church that was bombed during the Civil Rights movement, killing four young African American girls—Addie Mae Collins, Cynthia Wesley, Carole Robertson, and Carol Denise McNair.

In 1992, while I was pastoring in Birmingham and later serving as a chaplain in the Birmingham Fire Department, an imposing and stately limestone sculpture was dedicated in Kelly Ingram Park, known as the "Three Ministers Kneeling." The images in the sculpture are dressed in robes and kneeling in prayer, depicting John Thomas Porter, Nelson H. Smith, and Alfred Daniel Williams King (brother of Martin Luther King, Jr). On April 7, 1963, these men of faith, accompanied by peaceful marchers protesting the incarceration of Martin Luther King Jr., Ralph Abernathy, and Fred Shuttlesworth, were suddenly approached by law enforcement and instinctively knelt to pray on the sidewalk. Their audible and heartfelt prayers prevented what could have been a bloody Palm Sunday.

Prayer is the most urgent need in our lives, in the community, in the church, and in our nation as we seek to overcome inequity and injustice. That same power that worked on April 7, 1963, to restrain the evils of the day still works and should be embraced by those who believe in the power of an almighty God to both prevent and right wrongs.

Approximately one year following the dedication of the statute, I was honored to have been invited by Alabama United States Representative Tom Bevill (D), Alabama's 4th Congressional District, to serve as Guest Chaplain on June 17, 1993. It was a real honor to do publicly before the nation's lawmakers what I did privately each day. It was an even greater pleasure to have my family and future wife join me on this special occasion.

The excitement began when we arrived at the nation's capitol on a picture-perfect morning. The United States House of Representatives was called to order by the 49th Speaker of the United States House of Representatives, Thomas Foley (D), Washington's 5th Congressional District. His record on civil rights was impressive, as he had voted in favor of the Voting Rights Act of 1965, the Civil Rights Act of 1968, and the Civil Rights Restoration Act of 1987. Somehow, I sensed his desire to see this nation become a better place for all people. With total confidence in God's wisdom and power, I gave this prayer in the historical United States House of Representatives Chamber:

"Let us pray. Eternal God, whose mighty hands brought forth this world into existence, we acknowledge Your presence in the 20th century. We are cognizant of Your bountiful blessings upon this great nation, from the sandy beaches of the western coast to the majestic Appalachians. For these magnificent works, we duly exult Your name. In our quest for world peace and justice, we entreat Your divine guidance, for we are aware that You and You alone can restore universal tranquility and moral uprightness. We pray Your blessings of wisdom and understanding upon our President, members of Congress, and all others who render services to You through service to their country. As a nation, may we aspire toward peaceful relations with all other nations by giving the world an example of love, understanding, and devotion to Your cause and purpose. Amen." Congressional Record June 17, 1993, 103rd Congress.

Following the prayer, Representative Tom Bevill hosted my family for lunch in the Members' Dining Room, which is reserved for Representatives and their guests, and remarkably, a space that approximately one hundred years earlier would have prohibited African Americans from entering. We listened over lunch as Representative Bevill shared the rich history of the United States Capitol and how the United States Congress functions. It was very apparent during the conversation that Representative Bevill, as Speaker Foley, was interested in the advancement of all Americans, regardless of ethnicity.

It was a privilege to have prayed in the nation's capitol, that was built by slave labor, which was unacknowledged by earlier historians. Prior to its building, "George Washington and Thomas Jefferson were determined that the United States Capitol be a meaningful expression of America's new political and social order."[29]

The cornerstone was laid by Washington on September 18, 1793, and the architectural and interior design would showcase the spirit of freedom in America. It was determined that Europeans with artisan skills in constructing buildings with stones would be recruited and hired. However, there were difficulties getting workers transported to America. The contingency plan called for slave labor. "The Commissioners of the Federal District paid regional plantation owners for the use of their enslaved workforce; the owners pocketed the wages, while the commissioners provided housing, some medical care, and rations for all laborers under their watch."[30]

---

29 https://www.loc.gov/exhibits/uscapitol

30 https://www.whitehousehistory.org/enslaved-labor-and-the-construction-of-the-u-s-capitol

Prior to the building of the capitol, "In 1791 Pierre L'Enfant, who planned the City of Washington, leased African American slaves from their masters to clear the sites for the "President's House" and the Capitol."[31] Slaves worked in the quarry to cut stones for the capitol and government buildings. Women and children made bricks and were involved in all aspects of construction until the completion and the nation's capitol, that symbolized freedom, democracy, and liberty though freedom was far from their reach.

One such slave, Philip Reid, assisted his owner, Clark Mills, who was given the commission to cast Thomas Crawford's Statue of Freedom for the capitol's new dome. The Statue of Freedom is a female figure with long hair, wearing a helmet with the crest of an eagle's head and feathers. Her right-hand rests upon the handle of a sheathed sword wrapped in a scarf. In her left hand, she holds a laurel wreath of victory and the shield of the United States with 13 stripes. In the original drawing, she wore a Liberty Cap, which was a symbol of freedom and liberty over tyranny. In ancient Greece, this same symbol represented free men, such as Roman slaves who had been emancipated.

The United States Secretary of War, Jefferson Davis, later President of the Confederate States of America, was responsible for the construction of the capitol. He was an advocate of slavery and states' rights and opposed the Statue of Freedom's Liberty Cap, stating that "Its history renders it inappropriate to a people who were born free and should not be enslaved."[32] According to history, "The Red Phrygian or 'liberty' caps were long associated with the theme of liberty in European and colonial cultures. They were used as icons during the American Revolution and worn during the French Revolution."[33]

Davis was well informed of the history of the Liberty Cap but refused to change his position in order to not offend his Southern colleagues, who, like himself, owned slaves. However, Italian immigrant Constantino Brumidi, known for his work of painting the rotunda of the capitol, which includes "The Apotheosis of Washington" in the dome where George Washington is ascending to the heavens next to female figures; ironically, one of them is wearing a Liberty Cap.

When it was time to disassemble the plastered model of the Statue of Freedom for its bronze casting, Philip Reid was the only one identified as having the

---

31 https://www.archives.gov/press/press-releases/2001/nr01-30.html

32 https://www.aoc.gov/explore-capitol-campus/blog/liberty-cap-art-us-capitol

33 https://ageofrevolution.org/200-object/phrygian-cap/

knowledge and skills for the job. He skillfully separated the model so it could be moved to the foundry using a pulley and tackle to lift the figure without damaging it. "Without Reid, the plaster model of the statue might never have made it to the foundry." *Washington Post* April 16, 2014, Reid also assisted with the reassembly of the bronzed statue, which included working on weekends until it was finished. The irony of his life is that at the outset of working on the Statue of Freedom, he was a slave and not free, but he eventually received his freedom.

On December 18, 2007, the United States Congress passed legislation to name the Capitol Visitor Center's central space "Emancipation Hall" to remember the contributions of enslaved laborers who helped build the United States Capitol. In 2012, the United States Congress unveiled a marker to commemorate their role in building the United States Capitol. These men, women, and children deserve the long-overdue recognition for their roles in building America's temple of democracy. Whenever I see the capitol and admire its beauty and magnificence, I am also reminded that slaves played a significant role in its construction. Reid was like Bezalel, the chief artisan of the Tabernacle: The Lord said to Moses, "See, I have called by name Bezalel the son of Uri, the son of Hur, of the tribe of Judah. And I have filled him with the Spirit of God, in wisdom, in understanding, in knowledge, and in all manner of workmanship." (Exodus 31:2-3). God blessed these men with gifts and talent along with a willing heart.

The Power of a Praying Nation The Bible admonishes us to pray sincerely for our local, state, and national leaders (1 Timothy 2:1-4, Romans 13:1, 1 Peter 2:13-17). History reveals that our nation's founding fathers established a long-standing tradition of convening The Continental Congress, the legislative body that governed the United States from 1774 to 1789, with prayer. On September 7, 1774, Jacob Duché, Rector of Christ Church of Philadelphia, Pennsylvania, opened the Continental Congress with a passionate prayer: "look down in mercy, we beseech Thee, on these our American States, who have fled to Thee from the rod of the oppressor and thrown themselves on Thy gracious protection, desiring to be henceforth dependent only on Thee." America's prayer disposition should be applauded but does not make it a Christian nation.

The Founding Fathers such as James Madison, George Washington, John Adams, and Thomas Jefferson, varied on many issues, however, they agreed on the free exercise of religion and the separation of church and state. This freedom, including the freedom of religion, allows Christians in America to practice their faith openly and without fear. In Europe the royal houses and clergy considered those who opposed the church a threat to the state. Such was the case in England, "Many colonists came to America from England to escape religious persecution during the reign of King James I (r. 1603–1625) and of Charles I (r. 1625–1649)" https://www.mtsu.edu/first-amendment/article/1372/puritans#:~:text=Many%20colonists%20came%20to%20America,were%20hostile%20to%20the%20Puritans.

CHRISTIAN NATIONALISM

The question is often asked is America a Christian nation? According to the Pew Research Center "Six-in-ten U.S. adults – including nearly seven-in-ten Christians – say they believe the founders "originally intended" for the U.S. to be a Christian nation. And 45% of U.S. adults – including about six-in-ten Christians – say they think the country "should be" a Christian nation. A third say the U.S. "is now" a Christian nation." https://www.pewresearch.org/religion/2022/10/27/45-of-americans-say-u-s-should-be-a-christian-nation/

On the other side of the coin there are those who believe we should not attempt to elevate Christianity over another religion, nor legislate civil laws that reflect our view of Christianity. Further, while Christianity represents a belief in Christ Jesus, God has no preferred nations. However, "Christian nationalism is a political ideology and cultural framework that seeks to merge American and Christian identities." https://www.christiansagainstchristiannationalism.org/jan6report Although the United States Constitution is a secular document, it refers to religion in the First Amendment, which bars laws "respecting an establishment of religion or prohibiting the free exercise thereof," and in Article VI, which prohibits "religious tests" for public office. These provisions help to affirm the free exercise of religion without state interference.

An excellent starting point in our understanding of the wall of separation between church and state is the encounter Jesus had with the Herodians and Pharisees. This narrative is recorded in the three synoptic gospels (Luke 20:20–26; Mark 12:13–17; Matthew 22:15-22) and draws a sharp distinction between church and state. The religious leaders asked Jesus a potentially trap question: "Tell us, therefore, what do You think? Is it lawful to pay taxes to Caesar, or not?" Matthew 22:17 Jesus knew their motive and asked to see a coin, a denarius used to pay taxes, it was made of silver and featured an image of the emperor "Divine Caesar".

Jesus responded, "Render therefore to Caesar the things that are Caesar's, and to God the things that are God's." Matthew 22:21 Jesus emphasized compliance to the authority of the state and adherence to God's divine authority. The separation of the two institutions is designed to have a far-reaching positive impact on our democracy.

THE WALL OF SEPARATION

Through history, leaders of this nation have emphatically promoted the separation of church and state:

Future United States President James Madison on June 20, 1785, presented a document at the General Assembly of the Commonwealth of Virginia called the "Memorial and Remonstrance Against Religious Assessments". It was in opposition to Patrick Henry's Bill that proposed that "All Virginians be taxed to support "teachers of the Christian religion." https://presspubs.uchicago.edu/founders/documents/amendI_religions43.html

United States President George Washington, on August 18, 1790, wrote a letter to a Jewish congregation in Newport, R.I. Which affirmed the importance of protecting religious liberty and pluralism in America "The Citizens of the United States of America have a right to applaud themselves for having given to mankind examples of an enlarged and liberal policy: a policy worthy of imitation. All possess alike liberty of conscience and immunities of citizenship." https://www.au.org/wp-content/uploads/migration/pdf_documents/washingtons-letter-to-touro.pdf

On November 4, 1796, United States President John Adams reaffirmed that America is not a Christian Nation as he signed The Treaty of Tripoli (Treaty of Peace and Friendship between the United States of America and the Bey and Subjects of Tripoli of Barbary). The purpose of the treaty was to secure the protection of American ships in the Mediterranean Sea from local Barbary pirates. Tripoli (now Libya) was made aware that America had no intent to convert or colonize them, but only needed their protection from pirates.

Article 11 of the treaty stated: "As the government of the United States of America is not in any sense founded on the Christian Religion, as it has in itself no character of enmity against the laws, religious or tranquility of Musselmen, and as the said States never have entered into any war or act of hostility against any Mehomitan nation, it is declared by the parties that no pretext arising from religious opinions shall ever produce an interruption of the harmony existing between the two countries." https://www.mtsu.edu/first-amendment/article/2144/1797-treaty-of-tripoli

Finally on October 7, 1801, the Danbury Baptist Association in the State of Connecticut, wrote the newly elected United States President Thomas Jefferson concerning their continued protection of religious liberty as a minority faith group. Jefferson wrote to them " Believing with you that religion is a matter which lies solely between Man & his God, that he owes account to none other for his faith or his worship, that the legitimate powers of government reach actions only, & not opinions, I contemplate with sovereign reverence that act of the whole American people which declared that their legislature should 'make no law respecting an establishment of religion, or prohibiting the free exercise thereof,' thus building a wall of separation between Church & State." https://www.au.org/wp-content/uploads/migration/pdf_documents/JeffersonDanbury-Baptists.pdf

The actions of these men unequivocally affirm that America is not a Christian nation. However, it values the fervent prayers of its citizens from various faith traditions. According to the Congressional Research Service, June 23, 2014 "Although official prayers by public institutions are generally unconstitutional, there are a few notable exceptions. The Supreme Court has recognized that legislative prayer—invocations made to open legislative sessions—are generally permissible because of the role such prayers have played in the history and tradition of American government." https://sgp.fas.org/crs/misc/R43188.pdf

Following tradition, almost two hundred and twenty-five years later, while serving as a pastor in Tennessee, United States Senator William Frist (R), invited me to give the morning prayer in the United States Senate on June 17, 1999. It was a memorable occasion. My family, including my one-year-old son, joined me in the Russell Senate Office Building to have breakfast with Senator Frist and Dr. Lloyd John Ogilvie, then the chaplain of the United States Senate. As the conversation about national and world affairs progressed, I listened intently as both men shared the history and traditions of the United States Senate and the duties of the Senate Chaplain.

The time to fulfill my role as Guest Senate Chaplain came. Walking to the Senate floor of the upper chamber, the paintings, the furniture, and the beautiful decorum overwhelmed me. Waiting with God-dependent confidence as The President pro tempore Senator Strom Thurmond (R) of South Carolina convened the Senate, I stepped forward. Written several weeks earlier and approved by the Senate Chaplain, I petitioned God that historic day:

"Almighty God, who has worked through leaders of all ages to shape the events of history, we pray for the women and men in this Senate today. May they sense Your guiding providence and find wonder in the thought that You have chosen them through the voice of the American people to lead this mighty nation. While they are here in this historic chamber, remind them of their accountability to You for every choice which they shall make. May they live humbly and peacefully before You as they lead in making laws to govern our land. May they remember the limitations of human wisdom and power, and may they constantly rely on You, the omnipotent one, for strength and guidance. Dwell in the secret places of their hearts and grant them peace. Reveal Yourself to them; be the unseen Friend beside them in every changing circumstance. And may we all aspire for the day when "… Nation shall not lift up sword against nation, neither shall they learn war anymore" (Isaiah 2:4). Amen. Congressional Record June 17, 1999, 106th Congress.

The portrait of General George Washington when he served as commander of the Continental Army is one of my favorite paintings. Out of respect for General George Washington, his name runs throughout my ancestral lineage; my great grandfather, great uncle, father, son, and I bear the name Washington. The painting portrays Washington in the snow, kneeling reverently in prayer for his troops at Valley Forge in the winter of 1778.

Robert W. Pelton, in his book, *George Washington's Prayers*, shows that Washington dutifully recorded the words of advice his mother, Mary, gave him when he was leaving home to begin what would turn out to be a lifelong service to his country. She instructed her son with these words: "Remember that God is our only one trust. To Him, I commend you… My son, neglect not the duty of secret prayer."

The prayer came at a time when the British army seemed invincible. Washington's troops were exhausted, wet, and cold, living in huts with limited rations because merchants, shopkeepers, and farmers were hesitant to accept the Continental's currency as legal tender. So bad were the conditions that about 3,000 men died from typhus and dysentery, and other causes.

The outlook was dim for the Continental Army. In 1777, under Major General William Howe, the British Army had captured the jewel in the crown— Philadelphia, located only 25 miles west of where Washington's troops camped for the winter. During this period, loyalists to George III of England anticipated that the 13 colonies would break up; the legitimacy of the Continental Congress would come under scrutiny, and the voices of justice would grow silent. None of this happened, perhaps because of the prevailing power of General George Washington's prayer.

God has an unstoppable plan for this nation, which includes freedom of religion, the press, and speech, as well as peaceful protests. With the dawning of spring blooming of the cherry trees, hope renews in the hearts of the Continental Army soldiers, who concluded that their harsh winter had only been a test of dedication and commitment to fight for a worthy cause.

Providential events coincided with the melting of snow. Newly appointed Quartermaster General Nathanael Greene speedily constructed new roads and bridges to replenish the food and other commodities at Valley Forge. France's entry into the war on the Colonists' side was, perhaps, another providential occurrence. Encouraged by the course of events, General Washington and his troops marched back to the city of Brotherly Love and recaptured the city. Predictably, prayer was the difference-maker in this course of events. General George Washington did what we must all do without fail—he took a stand on his knees.

Twenty-two years later, at the end of more than twenty years of military service, I was most honored to have been invited by Alabama United States Senator Richard Shelby (R) to serve as Guest Chaplain in the United States Senate. I immediately acknowledged that the privilege of prayer comes from God, whether public or private. When we arrived at the capitol, my wife and I saw that the security was very restricted, as we had imagined after January 6, 2020, insurrection. We were greeted by two members of the senator's staff who escorted us through security to the office of Dr. Barry Black, the United States Senate chaplain.

Following an extremely warm visit with Dr. Black and his staff, my wife was accompanied to the senate seating gallery, and I walked with the chaplain to the senate floor as The President pro tempore, Senator Joseph Leahy (D) of Vermont, convened the Senate. With God-dependent confidence, I prayed this prayer for our nation:

"Almighty God, who reigns in splendor and majesty. We acknowledge Your divine power as we seek the blessings that will sustain and guide us through this day's journey. We pray that Your presence will fill this chamber and that You would grant our Senators sufficient wisdom, knowledge, and understanding with the deliberations and decisions that will be made. We thank you for this nation's indelible history and ask your blessings of protection upon it as we look forward to the glorious day that the Prophet Isaiah wrote about that proclaims: "He shall judge between the nations, And rebuke many people; They shall beat their swords into plowshares, And their spears into pruning hooks; Nation shall not lift up sword against nation, Neither shall they learn war anymore." (Isaiah 2:4 NKJV). This is my prayer in the name of Him that is eternal. Amen. Congressional Record May 12, 2022 117th Congress.

My gracious host, Dr. Barry Black, engaged me with many remarkable people who work tirelessly each day managing the affairs of the United States Senate, increasing my appreciation immensely for the commitment and dedication of those who serve in government. I was also reminded of the importance of prayer for government leaders, as admonished by St. Paul in 1 Timothy 2:1-4: "Therefore I exhort first of all that supplications, prayers, intercessions, and giving of thanks be made for all men, for kings and all who are in authority, that we may lead a quiet and peaceable life in all godliness and reverence. For this is good and acceptable in the sight of God our Savior, who desires all men to be saved and to come to the knowledge of the truth."

As the day concluded, these considerations prompted me to pray with both senators from Alabama (Richard Shelby (R) and Thomas Tuberville (R) during individual visits with them. I left the capitol feeling reassured that God is both watching over our nation and guiding its affairs. King David said it best in Psalm 22:8, "For the kingdom is the LORD's, And He rules over the nations."

There are some guidelines that I have found to be beneficial when praying in a government setting:

- The content of the prayer should be appropriate for the occasion and audience which is often comprised of diverse faith groups.

- Ensure grammatical and punctuation accuracy when making the written submission of the prayer.

- Inquire about the length of the prayer.

- Avoid references to specific deities, political parties, and issues.

- Pray with a natural voice and strong enunciation, but with sufficient projection for the physical space where the prayer is given.

- Practice reading the prayer audibly.

REFLECTING MORE ON THE TOPIC:

What were your most meaningful takeaways from this chapter?

____

____

____

____

What will you do differently because of your increased awareness?

____

____

____

____

What resources or support do you need to ensure the successful achievement of
your goals?

____

____

____

____

CHAPTER 3

VOTING—A RIGHT, DUTY, AND PRIVILEGE

At the end of World War II, my late father, Washington Johnson Sr., was honorably discharged after serving in the United States Army Air Corps as a medic. He and his three brothers made my grandmother incredibly proud of their valiant service to their country in three distinct branches of the armed forces. She regularly admired their handsomely decorated uniformed photos in a makeshift gallery created in her living room, where they were aligned on the wall by age, my father being the second oldest. The adventurous stories shared by my father and uncles over the years often kept me on the edge of my seat. They partially contributed to my inspiration to join the United States Navy Chaplain Corps.

One such story shared by my father left an unforgettable reminder of African Americans' daunting voter registration challenges. Following his military discharge in 1946, my father went to the Jefferson County courthouse in Birmingham, Alabama, to register to vote. Dressed professionally, as was his practice, he hoped his appearance would help to ease the voter registration process, which had become painstakingly challenging for African Americans in the South. He was asked to fill out a form, and he gladly completed it. However, the clerk seemed quite surprised at his literacy and proceeded to ask him additional questions about his background, even some that were not at all related to the voter registration process. Hopeful that the needless query would soon end and that his military service would advance him further in the voter registration process, he interjected that he had recently received an honorable discharge from the armed forces. continued asking questions unrelated to voting. My father refused to lower his dignity to answer the trap questions. Instead, he chose to wait in silence in what resembled a mini peaceful protest for what he knew was his right, duty, and privilege. Though the minutes of silence seemed like an eternity, my father became a registered voter. Many other African Americans who had served in the military to defend democracy, their country, and fellow citizens returned home to face similar instances of voter suppression.

During World War II, African Americans in southern states were still subject to Jim Crow laws, which set the stage for voter suppression and other injustices. The United States Armed Forces were segregated, including barracks, gyms, chapels, and dining facilities—all based on colorism. Ferris University's Jim Crow Museum of Racist Memorabilia: Using Objects of Intolerance to Teach Tolerance and Promote Social Justice paints an accurate picture of the Jim Crow racial caste system. The Ferris State University Jim Crow Museum of Racist Memorabilia[34] reported the following regarding Jim Crow:

The Jim Crow system was undergirded by the following beliefs or rationalizations: whites were superior to blacks in all important ways, including but not limited to intelligence, morality, and civilized behavior; sexual relations between blacks and whites would produce a mongrel race which would destroy America; treating blacks as equals would encourage interracial sexual unions; any activity which suggested social equality encouraged interracial sexual relations; if necessary, violence must be used to keep blacks at the bottom of the racial hierarchy. The following Jim Crow etiquette norms show how pervasive these practices were:

- A black male could not offer his hand (to shake hands) to a white male because it implied being socially equal. Obviously, a black male could not offer his hand or any other part of his body to a white woman because he risked accusations of rape.

- Blacks and whites were not supposed to eat together. If they did eat, serve whites first and place a partition between them.

- Under no circumstance was a black male to offer to light the cigarette of a white female—that gesture implied intimacy.

- Blacks were not allowed to show public affection toward one another in public, especially kissing, because it offended whites.

- Jim Crow etiquette prescribed those blacks were introduced to whites, never whites to blacks. For example: "Mr. Peters (the white person), this is Charlie (the black person), that I spoke to you about."

---

34 Ferris State University. (n.d.). What is Jim Crow? https://www.ferris.edu/jimcrow/what.htm

- Whites did not use courtesy titles of respect when referring to blacks, for example, Mr., Mrs., Miss., Sir, or Ma'am. Instead, blacks were called by their first names. Blacks had to use courtesy titles when referring to whites and were not allowed to call them their first names.

- If a black person rode in a car driven by a white person, the black person sat in the back seat or the back of a truck.

- White motorists had the right-of-way at all intersections[35].

Many other racist rules, unspoken and undocumented but enforced, stemmed from the Jim Crow system. One example my father shared occurred while stationed at Keesler Air Force Base in Biloxi, Mississippi.

There was an undocumented rule that African American service persons were not allowed to leave the base after dark. After my dad took a short leave during an Easter holiday weekend, his train returned late, placing him in violation of the unspoken curfew, which the local police department enforced. He contemplated his limited options of segregated hotels and knowing taxis would not patronize an African American soldier after sunset. His Christian acumen and values reminded him of the prayer his mother had petitioned earlier in the day for his safe arrival back to Mississippi, and he immediately sought divine intervention.

Suddenly, he heard a loud voice saying, "Hey, soldier! You will have to wait until tomorrow morning." As he looked around, he saw a police officer who continued with more directives, "You can sleep in one of the empty jail cells tonight." Though not an ideal solution, my father spent the night in the Biloxi City Jail. When I asked him if he was afraid to spend the night in jail, he responded, "The Lord sent his angels to protect me, and the next morning at sunrise, I was able to take the local bus back to the base with great relief."

POST-CIVIL WAR VOTER SUPPRESSION

While the Thirteenth Amendment officially abolished slavery, the new freedom granted to African Americans seemed all but mockery. Following the end of the American Civil War, federal officials and troops were strategically stationed throughout the southern states to administer policies for the wellness of former slaves. The Civil Rights Act of 1866 was one such policy. This legislation granted newly freed slaves the right to "make contracts, to own property, to sue

---

35 https://www.ferris.edu/jimcrow/what.htm

in court, and to enjoy the full protection of federal law."

One policy that some southerners opposed was allowing former slaves to vote and hold office. They used violence, the burning of churches and schools to intimidate former slaves and deter them from voting. In response, "The 15th Amendment to the United States Constitution reads "The right of citizens of the United States to vote shall not be denied or abridged by the United States or by any State on account of race, color, or previous condition of servitude." This Amendement was passed by the United States Congress February 26, 1869, and ratified February 3, 1870. The 15th Amendment granted African American men the right to vote. https://www.archives.gov/milestone-documents/15th-amendment "

Still, there would be a long road to voter equality, though some milestones during the Reconstruction Era (1865–1877) offered a glimmer of hope. Former slaves supported the Republican party because it was the party of Lincoln. Senator Hiram Revels of Mississippi and Representative Joseph Rainey of South Carolina became the first African Americans to serve in Congress—in seats that, just a decade earlier, were held by southern slave owners! The number of African Americans in public service increased over time, with many coming from the church, having worked as ministers during slavery or in the early years of Reconstruction. Approximately "2,000 African American men served in political office. Hundreds of blacks held local offices in the South, more than 600 were elected to state legislatures, and 16 served in Congress." https://blog.gale.com/asserting-equality-black-political-activism-during-reconstruction/#:~:text=During%20Reconstruction%2C%20about%202%2C000%20African,plagued%20by%20violence%20and%20fraud.

The African American church, prepared these men for their unprecedented leadership roles. From its emergence, the church has been an enduring haven in its community, not only for spiritual renewal, but during slavery, it brought hope through preaching and spirituals by turning their attention to the God who had liberated the Israelites from Egypt and instilling faith that He would do the same for them.

During the American Civil Rights Movement, the church became the center for planning strategies for peaceful protests against segregation and social injustice. Historically Black Colleges and Universities (HBCUs) such as Howard, Morehouse, Tuskegee, Hampton, and my own Alma Mater, Oakwood University, also played a pivotal role in the advancement of African Americans, educating scores of students for various professions. Then there are social action organizations such as the National Association for the Advancement of Colored People (NAACP), the Southern Christian Leadership Conference, and the Urban League that have contributed to the forward movement of African Americans.

THE COMPROMISE OF 1877

The 1876 presidential election produced no clear winner because neither candidate secured enough votes in the Electoral College to be declared President. A compromise, though unwritten, was made with Southern Democrats to settle this highly disputed election. Republican candidate Rutherford B. Hayes became the President in exchange for the withdrawal of federal troops in the South and the formal ending of the Reconstruction Era. The implications would prove to be far-reaching. The radical Reconstruction Era contributed to the restoration of the United States as a unified nation and the settling of the longstanding states' rights versus federalism issue. However, it fell short in other critical areas, as it did not produce the fundamental change needed in the South that would protect the freedoms granted to former slaves. Enactment of Black Codes from 1865 and 1866 "replaced the social controls of slavery removed by the Emancipation Proclamation and the Thirteenth Amendment to the Constitution."[36]

A few years later, in 1883, a very conservative Supreme Court declared the Civil Rights Act of 1875 as unconstitutional. This act was one of the last Reconstruction statutes, which had guaranteed African Americans equal treatment of public transportation, public accommodations, and the right to serve on juries. Over time, federal funds designated for Reconstruction programs shifted to other non-related projects. African Americans were again faced with circumstances akin to slavery, depriving them of basic citizenship rights that would inevitably include the right to vote or have equal representation in Congress.

In a collaborative effort and, seemingly, with a high degree of intentionality, Southern Governors and state legislators crafted a voter suppression system that continued into the 20th century. It included:

Poll taxes. A voting fee serves as a mechanism to deny African Americans the right to vote. The Poll Tax negatively impacted some Whites who could not afford the tax. Poll taxes were enacted in the 1890s and continued in Southern as well as some Northern states until 1964, when the twenty-fourth amendment prohibited poll taxes in federal elections.

Heightened law enforcement during elections resulted in threats, arrests,

36 https://www.britannica.com/topic/black-code

and heavy fines for African Americans who attempted to vote.

Economic reprisals Banks, landlords, and businesses reserved the right not to transact business with African Americans who voted. White Citizens' Councils strongly supported such actions, which would result in African Americans' removal from the election rosters.

Alabama's 1901 constitution, one of the strictest in voter suppression, required a poll tax and literacy test. However, it included a grandfather clause, which stated automatic registration if one's father or grandfather was registered.

Literacy tests, such as those in the State of Mississippi, required an applicant to read and interpret a section of the state constitution chosen by a local official.

Distribution of false information within the African American communities about voting precincts and alternative voting dates further inhibited African-Americans from participating in the voting process.

Even as of this publication, there is a growing wave of voter suppression bills. According to the Brennan Center for Justice, since "March 24, 2021, more than 361 bills that would restrict voting access have been introduced in 47 states."[37]

VOTERS SUPPRESSION 1960S / CIVIL RIGHTS ACT OF 1965

Voting honors those who sacrificed to achieve passage of the Voting Rights Act of 1965, which dismantled many barriers to voting rights. Men and women risked their lives so that African Americans could vote, some making the ultimate sacrifice. African American James Chaney (21) of Meridian, Mississippi, and his Jewish companions, Andrew Goodman (20) and Michael Schwerner (24) of New York City, were murdered by the Ku Klux Klan during "Freedom Summer" in 1964 in Mississippi.

Despite significant opposition, voters' rights campaigns continued. In 1965, the late congressman, John Lewis, attempted to lead 600 peaceful protestors across the Edmund Pettis Bridge in Selma, Alabama. In support of African Americans' right to vote, this march was to culminate in Montgomery, Alabama. State troopers used extreme violence to prevent the protestors from crossing the bridge. The event became known as bloody Sunday. Congressman Lewis suffered a fractured skull. Later, Dr. Martin Luther King Jr. and other clergy joined Lewis in successfully marching from Selma to Montgomery on March 21, 1965. Rabbi

---

37 https://www.brennancenter.org/our-work/research-reports/voting-laws-roundup-march-2021

Abraham Joshua Heschel described the march with these words. "For many of us, the march from Selma to Montgomery was about protest and prayer. Legs are not lips, and walking is not kneeling. And yet, our legs uttered songs. Even without words, our march was worship. I felt my legs were praying."[38]

These and other events paved the way for the passage of the Civil Rights Act of 1965, signed by United States President Lyndon Baines Johnson. This bill dismantled legal barriers to voting at the state and local levels. As a member of the White House Press Corps and executive editor of *Jet* magazine, my father's eldest brother, Robert Johnson Jr., witnessed the actual signing of the Civil Rights Act. My late uncle often reminded me of the tremendous responsibility that we, as beneficiaries of the untiring work, suffering, and sacrifices of those who fought for freedom, have. Despite the great sacrifices made for us to have voting rights, yet far too often, and for various reasons, the voting privilege goes unused.

ONE PERSON, ONE VOTE: VOTERS IDENTIFICATION AND GERRYMANDERING

Another crucial issue related to voter suppression among African Americans is the requirement for voter identification, which can often be difficult to obtain. Many minorities, underserved and elderly people, are unfamiliar with the complexity associated with securing personal identification and have subsequently negated the requirement as well as their right to vote. This has consequently discouraged voter turnout. It is reported that "25% of African-American citizens of voting age lack government-issued photo ID, compared to only 8% of whites."[39]

Another issue, though perhaps not viewed as voter suppression, is gerrymandering, which is an effort of some states to take away the authority of Secretaries of State, Governors, and nonpartisan election boards regarding the manner in which elections are run and votes counted. The debate of gerrymandering is almost as old as the nation. In 1790, the first United States census was taken during the Presidency of George Washington. The purpose of the constitutional mandate was to assess the growth and development of the nation. In 1812 Elbridge Gerry, who was the governor of Massachusetts and later Vice President of the United States, signed a Bill that created a partisan district in Boston that was shaped like a salamander. Governor Gerry's "administration was notable for its use of what became known as gerrymandering, the division of electoral districts for partisan political advantage."[40]

38 https://www.sefaria.org/sheets/114324?lang=bi

39 https://www.aclu.org/fact-sheet/oppose-voter-id-legislation-fact-sheet

40 https://www.britannica.com/biography/Elbridge-Gerry

Therefore, the term is associated with drawing or redrawing a congressional district favoring one party over the other. The apportionment is the appropriate term that is used for dividing the 435 seats in the United States House of Representatives among the 50 states. In most states, the state legislature has primary control of the redistricting process, both for state legislative districts and for United States Congressional districts. This process occurs every 10 years following a census and has an impact on which political party controls the United States Congress.

There are two methods that have been used to increase partisan control of congress. They are called packing, which allows as many voters as possible of an opposing party into one district, and cracking, which is splitting the opposing party's voters into many different districts. To address the issue of gerrymandering House Resolution.1, For the People Act of 2021 was introduced in the 117th United States Congress, which would "ban partisan gerrymandering, require all states to implement policies that would protect voting rights for communities of color, increase transparency and public participation in our elections, and implement independent redistricting commissions responsible for drawing fair maps."[41]

On March 3, 2021, the Bill passed in the United States Congress and later advanced to the United States Senate but lacked the 60 votes needed to invoke cloture after a party-line vote.

The future of gerrymandering is still an unsettled debate and will continue until common ground is found. In a democracy, voters should select their representatives and not representatives selecting their voters through the process of gerrymandering.

SHOULD PEOPLE OF FAITH VOTE?

The question is often asked: Should people of faith participate in voting considering the imminent return of Jesus? Can voting change the course of what the Bible forecasts about final events? Jesus' own words predict some of the worst of times to come. "The love of many shall wax cold" (Matthew 24:12). "And you will hear of wars and rumors of wars. See that you are not troubled, for all these things must come to pass, but the end is not yet. For nation will rise against nation, and kingdom against kingdom. And there will be famines, pestilences, and earthquakes in various places. All these are the beginning of sorrows." (Matthew 24:6-8).

---

41 https://indivisible.org/resource/fighting-gerrymandering-states

St. Paul, following the same train of thought, wrote, "But know this, that in the last days, perilous times will come: For men will be lovers of themselves, lovers of money, boasters, proud, blasphemers, disobedient to parents, unthankful, unholy, unloving, unforgiving, slanderers, without self-control, brutal, despisers of good, traitors, headstrong, haughty, lovers of pleasure rather than lovers of God, having a form of godliness but denying its power. And from such people turn away!" (2 Timothy 3:1-5)

These predictions are fast fulfilling without question but do not provide a legitimate reason for people of faith not to vote. The Bible also records the parable of the nobleman in Luke 19: 12-13: "A certain nobleman went into a far country to receive for himself a kingdom and to return. 13 So he called ten of his servants, delivered to them ten minas, and said to them, 'Do business till I come.'"

"Occupy till I come" is, in every sense, active and not passive. In other words, while anticipating the second coming, we are encouraged to be good stewards of the earth and promote society's wellbeing. Admonish members of the early Christian church to: "Let every soul be subject to the governing authorities. For there is no authority except God, and the authorities that exist are appointed by God." (Romans 13:1). Jesus Himself said, "Render therefore to Caesar the things that are Caesar's, and to God, the things that are God's." (Matthew 22:21). Voting represents both a privilege and responsibility that allows active participation in a democratic process that may not be perfect, but one that gives a voice to those who exercise voting rights.

CITIZENS OF TWO WORLDS

People of faith are considered citizens of two distinct worlds: the present earthbound world and the future world of eternity. They are called upon to embrace and operationalize the timeless values of eternity, as espoused in Micah 6:8: "He hath showed thee, O man, what is good; and what doth the LORD require of thee, but to do justly, and to love mercy, and to walk humbly with thy God?"

Carrying out this admonition allows us to function as "citizens of heaven" while living as citizens of this world. God's design is that Christians serve as the salt of the earth and light in what has become a dark world. About the salt, Jesus' words in Matthew 5:13 describe it as an active savoring agent to even be considered helpful in the earth: "Ye are the salt of the earth: but if the salt has lost his savor, wherewith shall it be salted? it is thenceforth good for nothing, but to be cast out, and to be trodden under foot of men." The God-given privilege of voting lends to the savoring work of making the present world the best it can be when positive change is the outcome. We have the responsibility to be informed voters and to vote for our convictions, our beliefs, and our values.

When a student at Oakwood University in 1980, I served as president of the NAACP college chapter. One of the organization's strategic goals was to promote voter registration and voter participation. Growing up, I understood the value of voting from what I had observed with my parents and other family members. The process began with the establishment of a relationship with the board of registrars. One must take special care to build up alliances with local election officials. The relational measures, complemented by much prayer and providential leading, helped pave the way for a successful voter registration drive.

Students needed transportation to the voting precincts; otherwise, the voter registration drive would have been fruitless. We hired a local bus service to transport students. The cost of $150 seemed quite expensive, but thanks to the generous donations of students and others on campus, we paid for it. It is easier to register to vote with today's technology, but the next generation must be as intentional as we were.

The efforts of the Oakwood University NAACP organization resulted in my being able to vote for the first time in the 1980 presidential election and many elections since then.

2020 PRESIDENTIAL ELECTION

With a sense of excitement and anticipation, my family and I were awakened on a chilly autumn morning by the golden sun's rays piercing through the windows. Mornings in our home had always been full of cheer; however, today had a unique feeling. What made November 3, 2020, so special? It was election day, and our son Washington Johnson III would be old enough to vote in his first presidential election. This experience would be symbolic due to three distinct family generations represented and sharing in the voting experience for the first time together. My 22-year-old son, a medical student at the historic Meharry Medical College, would be joined by his 90-year-old grandmother Dr. Mildred P. Johnson, who had lived through the Jim Crow South and Voters Right Act of 1965. November 3 would be the day they would both engage in carrying out their civic duty.

My wife and I shared with our son before reaching the polling site that voting was now his responsibility and to take it seriously. He understood that today was possible because of the pioneers of justice before him that had marched, stood, peacefully protested, and even died so that African Americans could vote. Therefore, voting holds much more significance than simply selecting a candidate on a paper ballot or touchscreen. It serves to call to remembrance the astronomical sacrifices made for the greater good of future generations, such as my son's.

As we reached the voting precinct, we marveled at the outpouring of community engagement, which was representative of all demographics. It was clear that this election was unlike any other, and the American people were intent on holding elected officials, regardless of their party affiliation, accountable. Although the precinct was exponentially crowded, the atmosphere was pleasant, and the lines moved surprisingly quickly. The experiences and feelings associated with that election morning will remain etched in our minds forever. After my son voted, he received the traditional sticker labeled with two words "I Voted." Despite the excitement, he eventually took the sticker off and continued with his pursuits. However, the meaning of these two simple words went far beyond the sticker. These two particular words embodied the incredible journey to equality that African Americans have endured in this country. A journey that is not yet complete but one in which people such as his grandmother understood far more than others would ever know.

Across the nation, voters stood in long lines, participated in early voting, or mailed in ballots that numbered more "than in any other election in U.S. history."[42] Those in the armed forces used absentee ballots. This process dates back to the American Civil War when Union soldiers were able to vote absentee in the 1864 presidential election, where incumbent President Abraham Lincoln of the National Union/Republican party defeated Democratic candidate General George McClellan with 55% of the popular vote and with 212 of 233 total electoral votes. "Alabama, Arkansas, Florida, Georgia, Louisiana, Mississippi, North Carolina, South Carolina, Tennessee, Texas, and Virginia did not participate in the election due to succession."[43]

Despite COVID-19, according to the *Washington Post,* November 5, 2020, "More Americans voted in the 2020 election than in any other in more than 100 years." There are several contributing factors for this truth, including the incumbent, President Donald Trump, generating enthusiasm among his sup-

---

42 https://time.com/5907062/record-turnout-history/

43 https://www.britannica.com/event/United-States-presidential-election-of-1864

porters and partisan races in which fewer people were undecided. Additionally, African Americans voting in large blocks in battleground states played a pivotal role in the outcome of the 2020 election. However, history will always reflect the turbulent events that followed. The incumbent, after losing the election, refused to accept the official state-certified results, especially in counties with high concentrations of people of color.

Although numerous failed attempts to undermine American Democracy are morally reprehensible, a loser's challenge after a fair election is legal because every vote should count and is counted in a democracy. The United States has always set the standard globally in our elections and peaceful transfer of power. On December 15, 2020, by majority votes in the Electoral College, Joseph Biden became the 46th President of the United States. The founding fathers were men with feet of clay, but God inspired them as they established this nation's check and balance system in the election process. While Americans are part of an ever-expanding mosaic of people who help to set the course of the nation's agenda through voting, God's providential leading is trustworthy even in election outcomes. Whether voting in a metropolitan city, a rural precinct in the Midwest, by mail or absentee, "for the kingdom is the Lord's, And He rules over the nations." (Psalm 22:28). However, the aftermath of the 2020 election would prove to result in one of the most catastrophic events in American history: an insurrection at the United States Capitol.

On January 6, 2021, the then-president gave what some might describe as a seditiously arousing speech to loyal supporters at a "March to Save America" rally at the Ellipse in President's Park, saying, "We will never give up, we will never concede,"[44] Based on unsubstantiated allegations of election fraud, then-President Trump, the losing candidate demands that the vice president and congress overturn the results of the 2020 general election. The gathered crowd proceeded to the United States Capitol, breaching security, breaking windows, trashing, and vandalizing the nation's symbol of democracy. At the same time, congress attempted to certify votes, mostly unaware of the seriousness of the insurrection. Social media flashed the horrific images of the insurrection, which traveled virally with unbelief around the globe. The assault on the United States Capitol was later widely condemned as "horrifying" and an "attack on democracy."[45]

During the insurrection, the capitol police evacuated the vice president

---

44 https://www.reuters.com/article/us-usa-election-trump/trump-says-we-will-never-give-up-we-will-never-concede-idUSKBN29B2BZ

45 https://www.bbc.com/news/world-us-canada-55568613 nationally and internationally

and members of the 117th United States Congress to an undisclosed area. They additionally secured the Senate and House of Representatives chambers and several other buildings in the Capitol complex. After the four hours of chaos, five people died, "including a Capitol police officer who was severally injured."[46]

Later that evening, congress reconvened to continue the counting, but now with combined protection from the Capitol Police, D.C. Metro Police, and DC National Guard. During the proceeding, some senators, as promised, objected to the certification of the general election, all based on unproven voting irregularities. However, in the early morning hours on January 7, 2021, the vice president (Mike Pence at the time) declared president-elect Joseph Biden and vice-president-elect Kamala Harris winners of the 2020 general election.

INAUGURATION DAY, JANUARY 20, 2021

The inauguration took place on the steps of the United States Capitol with many historical milestones, including the swearing-in of the oldest president-elect at seventy-eight years old and the first female vice president-elect. The nation's youth poet laureate, Amanda Gorman, twenty-two years old, delivered the inaugural poem, "The Hill We Climb," that included final lyrics penned the night after she had watched the horrific scenes of insurrection. The 2021 inauguration made history, as it differed from previous inaugurations in many ways: increased security resulting from the destructive actions of a pro-Trump mob a few days earlier; many coronavirus pandemic restrictions; a modified parade; and, finally, a virtual inaugural ball. A new tradition began as the president, and vice president traveled to Arlington National Cemetery to lay a wreath at the Tomb of the Unknown Soldier. Finally, according to historians, it was the first time since 1869 that the outgoing president did not attend the inauguration ceremony. "Andrew Johnson, the first U.S. President to be impeached, was also the last President to skip his successor's inauguration."[47]

Former President Donald Trump departed the White House before the inauguration ceremony. Former vice president, Mike Pence, remained to witness the peaceful transfer of presidential power. Despite the challenges of the 2020 presidential election, the United States is still a role model for democracy.

THE SELECT COMMITTEE: INVESTIGATION

January 6, 2020, will always be remembered as one of the darkest days in history because of the insurrection at the United States Capitol. Nancy Pelosi,

46 https://www.theguardian.com/us-news/2021/jan/08/capitol-attack-police-officer-five-deaths
47 https://time.com/5928537/trump-biden-not-attend-inauguration-history/

Speaker of the United States House of Representatives, proposed a commission to compile an account of what happened on this dreadful day and make recommendations to ensure the Capitol is never breached again. The bipartisan commission was designed to report the facts to both congress and the American people regarding the attack.

The chairman of the House Homeland Security Committee, Bennie Thompson (D), Mississippi's 2nd Congressional District, and its Republican ranking member, John Katko (R), New York's 24th Congressional District, reached an agreement on the creation of the panel. The House Republican Leader Kevin McCarthy appeared at first in favor, but later, he opposed the commission, stating, "Given the political misdirections that have marred this process… I cannot support this legislation."[48]

McCarthy withdrew all five picks and boycotted the panel.[49] The bill forming the commission passed the House on May 19, 2020; however, it was blocked in the Senate on May 28, 2020, failing to achieve the 60 votes required to break a filibuster.

Speaker Pelosi, in another effort to examine the events, stated, "This morning, with great solemnity and sadness, I am announcing that the House will be establishing a select committee on the Jan. 6 insurrection."[50] House Resolution 503 - Established the Select Committee to Investigate the January 6th Attack on the United States Capitol. Representatives Liz Cheney (R), Wyoming's at Large District, and Adam Kinzinger (R), Illinois's 16 Congressional District, were the only two House Republicans willing to serve on the committee, and the Republican National Committee eventually censured them for their participation. Despite the pushback, "The investigation commenced with public hearings on July 27, when four police officers testified. Since that time, the committee has "Interviewed nearly 1,000 people."[51]

The select committee subpoenaed White House communication records and former officials with close ties to the former president. Though the Republican

48 https://www.npr.org/2021/05/18/997836874/top-house-republican-opposes-bipartisan-commission-to-probe-capitol-riot

49 https://www.politico.com/news/2022/05/02/subpoena-rnc-records-capitol-riot-00029265

50 https://www.npr.org/2021/06/24/1009818514/house-speaker-nancy-pelosi-launches-select-committee-to-probe-jan-6-insurrection

51 https://www.pbs.org/newshour/politics/after-nearly-a-thousand-interviews-jan-6-panel-considers-calling-trump-and-pence

National Committee insisted that the committee was invalid and should not be allowed to investigate, the select committee will ultimately finalize a report that will reveal to the nation what happened and how future occurrences can be avoided. The founding fathers would be puzzled by the events of that fateful day. They had differences even on slavery, but they collectively envisioned the larger picture that it was critical to form a nation on the principles of democracy as a counter to tyranny.

Benjamin Franklin was asked after the Constitutional Convention what form of government we will have, and he replied, "A republic if you can keep it." The United States was close to losing its democracy on January 6 as the insurrectionists attempted to overturn the will of the people. In a democracy, there are checks and balances to safeguard the rights of all people. Any attempt to do otherwise would go against the grain of democracy.

EXECUTIVE SUMMARY: SELECT COMMITTEE

On December 19, 2022, the bi-partisan January 6 Select Committee, after 18 months, met to vote on potential recommendations to the Justice Department. Chairman Representative Bennie Thompson said. "We have every confidence that the work of this committee will help provide a roadmap to justice."[52]

Representative Liz Cheney, in her opening statement, said, "Every president in our history has defended this orderly transfer of authority—except one,"[53] The bi-partisan committee voted 9-0 to approve its final report and "concluded that former President Donald Trump was ultimately responsible for the insurrection."[54] The report outlined step by step how former President Trump attempted to remain in power. History will be the judge of his actions and will be decided if the actions taken and decisions made were right or wrong. Time heals some wounds, but scars will not completely fade away, which is the case with the insurrection of January 6, 2021.

---

52 https://www.npr.org/2022/12/20/1144303656/5-takeaways-from-the-final-jan-6-committee-hearing

53 https://www.newsweek.com/liz-cheney-praised-after-last-jan-6-speech-holding-back-no-punches-1768238

54 https://www.cnn.com/2022/12/19/politics/what-is-in-jan-6-committee-report-summary/index.html

REFLECTING MORE ON THE TOPIC:

What were your most meaningful takeaways from this chapter?

____

____

____

____

What will you do differently because of your increased awareness?

____

____

____

____

What resources or support do you need to ensure the successful achievement of your goals?

____

____

____

____

CHAPTER 4

ADVOCATE FOR JUSTICE

During the summer of my first year in college, a friend spent several weeks with my family in Birmingham, Alabama. He was from Pennsylvania and was astute in politics and social justice issues. One day he said to my brother and me, "There is a Ku Klux Klan rally today, and we need to check it out." I thought for a moment, and then my curiosity overruled all else, and I responded, "Let's go!" The three of us packed into his black Volkswagen, intentionally concealing our plans, especially from our parents, who would have wisely counseled us to avoid this event. Still dressed for church, we removed our neckties and jackets in sync to assimilate in the crowd but were careful to stay close together. The rally was what we had expected. A Klansman dressed in a white robe and hood spoke through a bullhorn to an enthusiastic crowd of ordinary-looking people. It was pretty surprising to see an audience of people you would see at a football game, the grocery store, or working in government or other professional organizations. Some proudly waved their Confederate flags; others held insulting signs.

The speaker's message was anti- "everything," with a running theme honoring Nathan Bedford Forrest, a Confederate General during the American Civil War who later served as "The first grand wizard of the Ku Klux Klan during the early years of Reconstruction."[55]

After two hours of intense listening, we agreed it was time to leave. We discussed the rally with deep regret that such an event would take place in a city considered the cradle of the American Civil Rights Movement. On the other hand, we realized that the Klansman had a right to express their views, as guaranteed in the 1st Amendment of the United States Constitution: "freedom of religion, speech, press, assembly, and petition."[56] It is a privilege to live in a

---

55 https://www.britannica.com/biography/Nathan-Bedford-Forrest

56 https://constitutioncenter.org/interactive-constitution/amendment/amendment-i

nation where people can peacefully protest or advocate for any issue that they deem essential.

THE PARADOXICAL WORDS OF PATRICK HENRY

Throughout our nation's history, advocates for justice have expressed their willingness to pay the ultimate price for freedom "Give me liberty or give me death!"[57] These memorable words were spoken by Patrick Henry during his speech on March 23, 1775, at the St. John's Church in Richmond during the Virginia Convention. Henry's audience consisted of legislators who were landowners and members of Virginia's aristocracy, whose wealth was built upon the system of slavery. His words, "Give me liberty or give me death!" represented an urgent call to arms against tyranny as their rights of freedom and liberty were under attack. These words, however, were not meant for slaves who were considered as property.

Henry was a man of faith, known for his arousing speeches where he often used biblical references to make his argument. Perhaps this can be attributed to listening to preachers in his youth when attending religious revivals with his mother during the Great Awakening. He championed religious freedom and opposed slavery in the colonies. However, he struggled with the question of slavery throughout his life. Henry was born in Virginia, "Old Dominion," where slavery was a necessity to the economy as tobacco became a major cash crop. Upon his marriage to Sarah Shelton, her father gave the couple a wedding gift of a"600-acre farm called Pine Slash and six slaves."[58]

Henry, in his heart, embraced the many principles of the abolitionists and even referred to slavery as a "lamentable evil."[59]

After reading a book written by Anthony Benezet opposing slavery, he responded, "He couldn't find a way to suffer the inconvenience of not having enslaved people around to do his bidding."[60]

Another struggle was his opposition to the ratification of the United States Constitution, which was a source of conflict between him and Thomas Jefferson. Henry felt that the United States Constitution put too much power in the hands of a national government. However, the Bill of Rights, the first 10 Amendments to the United States Constitution, guaranteed civil rights and liberties to all

57 https://avalon.law.yale.edu/18th_century/patrick.asp

58 https://encyclopediavirginia.org/entries/henry-patrick-1736-1799/

59 https://teachingamericanhistory.org/document/patrick-henry-to-robert-pleasants/

60 https://medium.com/black-history-month-365/give-me-liberty-or-give-me-death-b25a736dd903

citizens. They were inspired by Thomas Jefferson and drafted by James Madison. Both men were Virginians and would later become presidents of the United States.

Though he served as Governor of Virginia on several occasions and was involved in his law practice, the subject of slavery was a steady thorn in his side. In a letter written to Robert Pleasants, a Quaker, and an abolitionist, he said, "I claim to be a Christian, and no legitimate Christian can support the institution of slavery."[61]

Henry treated his slaves differently from other slave owners as he taught them to read the Bible and useful trades. However, they never experienced the freedom or liberty he so loudly touted.

By the time of Henry's death, his six gifted slaves had grown to sixty-seven slaves who were willed to his wife and sons as property, further perpetuating the inhumane and soul-crushing institution of slavery. His famous words, "Give me liberty or give me death!" Were totally unaligned with his behavior.

Equality is a core element of our nation's framework; equal opportunities exist for all citizens, including "Life, Liberty, and the pursuit of Happiness." These "unalienable rights" in the United States Declaration of Independence are natural—the right to exist, question, and own property—all legal rights that provide a semblance of civility. Yet, America's history records that slaves did not enjoy these fundamental rights on the premise that slaves were the property of their owners.

In 1857, Dred Scott hoped to obtain these rights when he sued for his freedom after spending time in a free territory. Chief Justice Roger Taney of the United States Supreme Court ruled against him on the basis that "African Americans could not sue in federal court because they could not be citizens of the United States."[62]

The verdict was not surprising since Taney himself was "a former slave owner, as were four other southern justices on the Court."[63]

The Declaration of Independence established the country's national aspira-

---

61 https://www.governing.com/context/a-dose-of-liberty-after-death-for-patrick-henry

62 https://www.britannica.com/event/Dred-Scott-decision

63 https://www.ushistory.org/Us/32a.asp

tions, and the Constitution was the channel through which the process happened. Immigrants came to America with the dream of experiencing economic, political, and social freedoms inconceivable in their countries. However, the Dred Scott case showed that American democracy did not envision slaves having rights. The enslaved entered a life of servitude without an exit clause. This inhumanity inspired the abolitionist movement.

In the northeast, abolitionists advocated through newspaper articles, public forms, and the pulpit, against slavery in the South. Prominent voices such as Sojourner Truth, Frederick Douglass, William Lloyd Garrison, and Harriet Beecher Stowe lifted their voices in perfect harmony, supporting social justice.

BIBLICAL FRAMEWORK FOR SOCIAL JUSTICE

Answers to every question related to social justice can be found in the Bible. The words written in Micah 6:8 represent the foundation on which Christians should embrace social justice: "He has shown you, O man, what is good; And what does the Lord require of you But to do justly, To love mercy, And to walk humbly with your God?" Micah 6:8 This verse proclaims what is required of Israel and it is also an introduction to a covenant lawsuit brought by God, the plaintiff, against Israel, the defendant.

COVENANT LAWSUIT

The concept of a covenant lawsuit is associated with German theologian, Hermann Gunkel, who is also credited as being the first scholar to isolate and analyze the literary form of "prophetic lawsuit." https://digitalcommons.andrews.edu/cgi/viewcontent.cgi?article=2949&context=pubs

The book of Genesis records the ancient practice of "cutting" a covenant which was customary among the Hittites in the ancient Near East. After the cutting process, "... two parties who were to be bound by a covenant walked between the halves of the animals." https://ready4eternity.com/the-bizarre-story-of-abraham-cutting-animals-in-half/ God cut a covenant with Abraham "So He said to him, "Bring Me a three-year-old heifer, a three-year-old female goat, a three-year-old ram, a turtledove, and a young pigeon." Then he brought all these to Him and cut them in two, down the middle, and placed each piece opposite the other; but he did not cut the birds in two." Genesis 15:9-10

Old Testament history records that Israel was disloyal to the covenant made between God and the Patriarch Abraham. The covenant that God made with Abraham was to extend to his posterity: "Look now toward heaven, and count the stars if you are able to number them." And He said to him, "So shall your descendants be." Genesis 15:5 While the blessings to Abraham's heirs were promised in abundance, they were conditional upon their faithfulness and obedience to God's law and doing justly toward others. Among many other reminders of God's faithfulness and requirements for obedience, prior to the Israelites entering Canaan, Moses said, "Therefore know that the Lord your God, He is God, the faithful God who keeps covenant and mercy for a thousand generations with those who love Him and keep His commandments." Deuteronomy 7:9

As if the reminders fell on death ears, Israel became like the nations around them overtime by oppressing the poor, engaging in adulterous practices, and neglecting the vulnerable. Both parties were summoned, and heaven and earth were appointed judges. The indictment included, but was not limited to economic injustice, immorality, and outright rebellion against worship of God "The rich were living in luxury while the marginalized suffered to pay for extravagances for those in power." https://www.westmont.edu/why-micah-6-8#:~:-text=Micah%206%3A8%20is%20a,of%20justice%2C%20reconciliation%20and%20diversity The guilty verdict was substantiated by conclusive evidence of the breach of the covenant. Ironically, The Israelites themselves had experienced slavery in Egypt as God had revealed to Abraham during the covenant ceremony. The Lord said "Know certainly that your descendants will be strangers in a land that is not theirs, and will serve them, and they will afflict them four hundred years. And also the nation whom they serve I will judge; afterward they shall come out with great possessions." Genesis 15:13-14

However, human nature has a pattern, seemingly quoted quite well by Paulo Freire in his book, *Pedagogy of the Oppressed*: "The oppressed, instead of striving for liberation, tend themselves to become oppressors." The Christian community must stand in solidarity against any form of injustice that systematically humiliates a people. It is equally important to act justly, as we all have been justified through Jesus Christ: "Therefore, having been justified by faith, we have peace with God through our Lord Jesus Christ." Romans 5:1 Jesus' mission to earth was to restore humanity's broken relationship with the Father. Therefore, we MUST live out Micah 6:8 in our daily lives as spiritual children of Abraham.

The Hebrew word for justice in Micah 6:8 is *mishpat*, which, more than 200 times in the Old Testament, means punishment or retributive justice. It also includes seeking out the vulnerable and treating all people fairly and as they deserve. Micah is joined by multiple biblical passages (Isaiah 1:17; Proverbs 31:9; Zechariah 7:9-10; Jeremiah 22:3; Romans 12:15-18; Provers 31:8-9; Psalm 9:9,

Psalm 82:3; Luke 10:30-37; Matthew 7:12; 1John 3:17-18; Leviticus: 19:15; James 1:27; Luke 4:18-19; Amos 5:24; Amos 5:11-15; Isaiah 59:6-12; Ezekiel 16:49-50; Matthew 19:21; Proverbs 29:7; Deuteronomy 16:20; Proverbs 14:31; Matthew 25:31-46,) that make social justice a mandate of faith.

JUSTICE IN THE TORAH

In the Old Testament, Moses amplified advocacy of justice for the disenfranchised and marginalized:

Economic injustice: "You shall not charge interest to your brother—interest on money or food or anything that is lent out at interest." (Deuteronomy 23:19). This includes victimization of the poor through payday advances and salary loans that charge exorbitant interest rates.

Feeding the hungry "When you reap your harvest in your field and forget a sheaf in the field, you shall not go back to get it; it shall be for the stranger, the fatherless, and the widow, that the LORD your God may bless you in all the work of your hands." (Deuteronomy 24:19-20, Leviticus 23:22).

Food insecurity is defined by the United States Department of Agriculture's Economic Research Service (ERS) as "…households that were uncertain of having, or unable to acquire, enough food to meet the needs of all their members because they had insufficient money or other resources for food." Seniors are especially impacted by food insecurity. "In 2020, nearly 9.5 million adults ages fifty and older were food-insecure. Five million of them were sixty or older."[64]

According to the United States Department of Agriculture's Economic Research Service In 2021:

33.8 million people lived in food-insecure households.

8.6 million adults lived in households with very low food security.

5.0 million children lived in food-insecure households in which children, along with adults, were food insecure.

521,000 children (0.7 percent of the Nation's children) lived in households in which one or more children experienced very low food security.[65]

According to the United States Department of Agriculture, in 2021, nearly

---

64 https://www.aarp.org/ppi/info-2022/boosting-snap-participation-among-older-adults.html

65 https://www.ers.usda.gov/topics/food-nutrition-assistance/food-security-in-the-u-s/key-statistics-graphics/

20% of Black individuals lived in food-insecure households. In addition, Blacks are almost three times as likely to face hunger as Whites. Black children are more likely to experience hunger than children of other races. In 2021, the United States Department of Agriculture reported that 22% of Black children lived in food-insecure households. Black children were almost three times as likely to face hunger as white children.

Surprisingly, rural residents face food insecurity to a similar degree as Urban residents based on limited access to affordable and healthy food choices. According to the United States Department of Agriculture, in 2021, 11% of rural households were food insecure, compared to households in metropolitan areas (12.2 percent) according to the United States Department of Agriculture, in 2021. Driving to a competitive supermarket from a rural area is challenging, causing residents to purchase unhealthy foods sold at convenience stores or gas stations.

INJUSTICE IN THE COURT SYSTEM

"For the Lord, your God is God of gods and Lord of lords, the great God, mighty and awesome, who shows no partiality nor takes a bribe. He administers justice for the fatherless and the widow and loves the stranger, giving him food and clothing. Therefore love the stranger, for you were strangers in the land of Egypt." (Deuteronomy 10:17-19).

"Cursed is the one who perverts the justice due the stranger, the fatherless, and widow. And all the people shall say, 'Amen!'" (Deuteronomy 27:19).

"Do not oppress the widow or the fatherless, The alien or the poor. Let none of you plan evil in his heart Against his brother." (Zachariah 7:10).

"Who executes justice for the oppressed, Who gives food to the hungry. The Lord gives freedom to the prisoners. The Lord opens the eyes of the blind; The Lord raises those who are bowed down; The Lord loves the righteous. The Lord watches over the strangers; He relieves the fatherless and widow; But the way of the wicked He turns upside down." (Psalm 146:7-9).

"Open your mouth for the speechless, In the cause of all who are appointed to die. Open your mouth, judge righteously, And plead the cause of the poor and needy." (Proverbs 31:8-9).

Despite these brief biblical commands, there are notable injustices in the American court system. African Americans, in particular, are incarcerated at a significantly higher rate than others, 5.1 times higher than the imprisonment of Whites in state prisons. "In five states (Iowa, Minnesota, New Jersey, Vermont, and Wisconsin), the disparity is more than 10 to 1." In many cases, they cannot afford legal counsel and depend on court-appointed attorneys.[66]

The privatized prison system in the nation has developed into a business corporation model with the goal of producing a profit. According to the National Institute of Corrections, "Since 2000, the number of people housed in private prisons has increased 32% compared to an overall rise in the prison population of 3%."[67]

Currently, "A total of 26 states and the federal government use private corporations."[68] It is commonly known that "These private prisons have also been linked to numerous cases of violence and atrocious conditions."[69] There are state legislators who believe that privatizing prisons is cost-effective and should replace state-run prisons. However, the "Three primary purposes of prisons are being a deterrent to crime, a punishment to the criminal, and to rehabilitate the criminal."[70] The profits gained from privatized prisons should not be prioritized ahead of prisoners' safety, health, and humane living conditions.

Another issue related to the privatized prison system is the outsourcing of prisoners to other states—in some cases, without the knowledge of the judge. This can be a financial and mental strain on families traveling hundreds of miles to visit with inmates. According to Emma Kaufman, Assistant Professor at New York University Law School, "Under current doctrine, prisoners have no right to be incarcerated in the state where they were convicted, and states may trade prisoners—either for money or for other prisoners—when they wish."[71]

While prison outsourcing may be legally carried out among states, this can result in disproportionate numbers of incarcerated African Americans in certain states since this population makes up approximately "38.6% of the United States prison population."[72] States that initiate outsourcing might reflect lower

---

66 https://www.sentencingproject.org/publications/color-of-justice-racial-and-ethnic-disparity-in-state-prisons/ June 14, 2016

67 https://nicic.gov/private-prisons-united-states-2021

68 https://www.sentencingproject.org/reports/private-prisons-in-the-united-states/

69 https://www.aclu.org/issues/smart-justice/mass-incarceration/private-prisons

70 https://federalcriminaldefenseattorney.com/the-purpose-of-prison-and-the-measuring-stick-of-recidivism/

71 https://www.law.nyu.edu/news/ideas/prisoner-trade-criminal-justice-emma-kaufman

72 https://www.bop.gov/about/statistics/statistics_inmate_race.jsp

numbers of incarcerations, giving an inaccurate reflection of crimes committed in those states. Outsourcing prisoners is like the energy world with buying "energy credits" and then claiming to "be green" while being a polluter. These dismal statistics should prompt focused, compassionate and determined action by those willing to embrace biblical social justice: (see also Amos 6, Jeremiah 22, Isaiah 58; Isaiah 1, Leviticus 19, Leviticus 25). The same can include:

- Advocating for the rights of those without a voice until their voices are empowered.
- Defending persons who are too helpless to defend themselves.

- Courageously modeling and speaking up for what is right and proper in God's eyes.

The question is often asked, "how can I respond and get involved in supporting social justice?" These strategies can prove to be most beneficial for igniting involvement in social justice issues:

1. Examine personal biases - Biases, both implicit and explicit, impact the way interactions occur with others. The lack of awareness greatly hinders the confrontation of biases and can result in blind spots over a lifetime. Mahzarin Banaji and Anthony Greenwald, in the book, *Blindspot* (2013), describe the mind as an automatic association-making machine where whatever it encounters, something related usually comes to mind. However, many people are victims of what Banaji and Greenwald (2013) describe as "Mind Bugs," or ingrained habits of thought that lead to errors in how we perceive, remember, reason, and make decisions. This sets the stage for biased thinking, which could continue throughout a lifetime if there is no self-awareness or attention given to the condition. Further, if biases are ignored, people can find themselves exclusively surrounded by people who think, look, and act the same as themselves. Authentic commitments to social justice, diversity, and inclusion require that every effort is made to see the best in others without partiality. When we sincerely pray for power to embrace others and treat them with dignity and respect, we are embracing the Scriptures, which teach impartiality.

"You shall do no injustice in judgment. You shall not be partial to the poor nor honor the person of the mighty. In righteousness, you shall judge your neighbor." (Leviticus 19:15).

"For the Lord your God is God of gods and Lord of lords, the great God, mighty and awesome, who shows no partiality nor takes a bribe." (Deuteronomy 10:17).

"Let me not, I pray, show partiality to anyone; Nor let me flatter any man." (Job 32:21).

"For there is no partiality with God." (Romans 2:11).

"I charge you before God and the Lord Jesus Christ and the elect angels that you observe these things without prejudice, doing nothing with partiality." (1 Timothy 5:21).

2. Educate - Self-awareness and examination is ideally followed by education of self on social justice issues. This can occur through the study of the history of social justice and researching organizations that are actively involved in the movement. Much can also be learned by engaging with social justice advocates, viewing documentaries regarding social justice, and attending meetings sponsored by organizations that promote social justice.

3. Volunteer - Volunteering costs nothing but time and authentic commitment to seeing positive change. It will significantly improve knowledge and understanding of the social justice movement and may require stepping outside of one's comfort zone. For example, it may involve entering an environment where you are the minority. However, comfort increases immensely as authenticity and commitment are developed and sustained in volunteer settings.

4. Social Media - is a proven platform that can be used to build strong networks with groups and organizations dedicated to social justice. Social media allows blogging, postings, discussion facilitation, and sharing of resources in real-time. Social justice advocacy is under-addressed and deserving of ample focus on social media platforms.

5. Financial Support - is greatly needed by many organizations that advocate for social justice and is a great way to get involved. However, it is important to visit the official websites of respective organizations and request financial records to determine if the organization is deemed legitimate before contributing. Contributions are also taxable in most cases.

Finally, there are many faith-based and non-faith-based organizations that are committed to ending mass incarceration, criminal justice reform, and protecting human liberties. Social justice should be nonpartisan, ensuring that all people, regardless of their socioeconomic status, are entitled to equal justice.

ESTHER

The classic story of Esther offers a most fitting example of courageous advocacy for justice, empowerment, and liberation.

As the story goes, Haman, a descendant of Agag, king of the Amalekites, became the Prime Minister of Persia and devised a scheme "to annihilate the Jews that were in the Persian Empire.

Esther's cousin, Mordecai, said to her, "who knows whether you have come to the kingdom for such a time as this?" (Esther 4:14). She was endowed with a power that she had never exercised in her queenly role; neither had she leveraged her position to maneuver others into power or produced a male heir who might make her position more advantageous.

However, upon recognizing the need for urgent and necessary action, Esther agreed to advocate for her people. At the risk of her own life, she made an unannounced visit to her husband, King Xerxes of Persia, who granted her wish to spare the lives of her people.

Haman, the official who perpetrated the injustices against the Jews, was himself treated justly by being hanged on the gallows he had built for Mordecai. The story of Esther affirms the importance of advocacy as a means of making positive change for the good of others.

JESUS AND SOCIAL JUSTICE/THE NEW TESTAMENT

The ministry of Jesus in the Gospels reveals that He often met people's physical needs before addressing their spiritual ones.

Luke 4:18-19 gives an overview of His mission, which fulfills the prophecy of Isaiah 61:1. As the anointed Messiah, Jesus preached an inclusive message of liberation, restoration, and deliverance. "The Spirit of the Lord is upon Me because He has anointed Me to preach the gospel to the poor; He has sent Me to heal the brokenhearted, to proclaim liberty to the captives And recovery of sight to the blind, To set at liberty those who are oppressed; To proclaim the acceptable year of the Lord." (Luke 4:18-19)

Christ was an advocate for justice. He broke down socio-economic, cultural, and religious barriers. Christ preached the gospel to the poor, to those destitute of the comforts of life, as well as to the brokenhearted, consoling persons experiencing internal and external pain. He also restored both physical and spiritual sight to the blind and proclaimed liberty to the captive.

JESUS—AN ADVOCATE FOR ALL

Women: Jesus was inclusive of women and placed a high value on them. He conversed with the Samaritan woman at Jacob's well (John 4), and He elevated women by referring to them as "daughters of Abraham" (Luke 13:16). Jesus instantly healed the woman who touched the hem of His garment (Mark 5:25-34); He had compassion on the mothers who brought their children to Him to be blessed (Matthew 19:14).

Race and ethnicity: Jesus miraculously healed the Syrophoenician (Canaanite) woman's daughter (Matthew 15:21-28; Mark 7:24–30). In the story of the good Samaritan, Jesus illustrated the nature of true religion that reaches beyond church walls, finding its roots in the soil of acceptance and compassion for all people, regardless of race, color, religion, or creed Luke 10:35-37.

The physically challenged, Poor, and Sick: John the Baptist, while imprisoned, was not confident of his future and sent his disciples to confirm if Jesus was the Messiah. "Jesus answered and said to them, "Go and tell John the things which you hear and see: The blind see, and the lame walk; the lepers are cleansed, and the deaf hear; the dead are raised, and the poor have the gospel preached to them. And blessed is he who is not offended because of Me." (John 11:4-6). Through His miracles, Jesus showed love, compassion, and empathy for those who were disadvantaged:

Two blind men healed Matthew 9:27-31.

Healing the paralyzed man John 5:1-8.

Healing the woman with an infirmity John 13:10-17.

Healing the ten lepers (Luke 17:11-19).

Healing the nobleman's son of fever (John 4:46-54).

Feeding the four thousand (Matthew 15:32-39; Mark 8:1-9).

Healing the centurion's servant of palsy (Matthew 8:5-13; Mark 7:1-10).

Healing the man with the withered hand (Matthew 12:9-13, Mark 3:1-5, Luke 6:6-11).

Feeding the five thousand Matthew (14:15-21, Mark 6:32-44, Luke 9:11-17, John 6:1-13).

Jesus lived by the New Testament Message of Social Justice:

"You shall love your neighbor as yourself." (Matthew 22:39).

"And the King will answer and say to them, 'Assuredly, I say to you, inasmuch as you did it to one of the least of these My brethren, you did it to Me.'" (Matthew 25:40).

"Pure and undefiled religion before God and the Father is this: to visit orphans and widows in their trouble, and to keep oneself unspotted from the world." James 1:27.

"Rejoice with those who rejoice, and weep with those who weep. Be of the same mind toward one another. Do not set your mind on high things, but associate with the humble. Do not be wise in your own opinion. Repay no one evil for evil. Have regard for good things in the sight of all men. If it is possible, as much as depends on you, live peaceably with all men." Romans 12:15-18.

THEOLOGY OF LIBERATION

The concept of Black Liberation theology is the bedrock of social justice. It is attributable to the writings of the late African American systematic theologian Dr. James Cone, often referred to as the father of Black Theology. Cone, a practitioner at Union Theological Seminary, is also the author of the 1970 publication, *A Black Theology of Liberation*, based on the Old Testament, anchors his writings on the belief that God takes the side of the oppressed. One such story is God's liberation of the Israelites from slavery (Exodus 7). Similarly, Cone embraced the belief that the "New Testament revealed Jesus as one who identified with those suffering under oppression, the socially marginalized and cultural outcasts."[73]

Other theologians also embrace the tenets of Liberation Theology. Howard Thurman, a theologian, educator, and mentor of Dr. Martin Luther King Jr, believed that Jesus understood oppression firsthand, having been born during the Roman occupation of Palestine. "Jesus was not a Roman citizen. He was not protected by the normal guarantees of citizenship—that quiet sense of security which comes from knowing that you belong and the general climate of confidence which it inspires."[74]

During the Roman occupation by law, a Roman citizen or soldier could

---

73 https://en.wikipedia.org/wiki/Black_theology

74 Jesus and the Disinherited page 33

compel a subject from a conquered nation to carry their bags one mile. Jesus addressed this inequity in His Sermon on the Mount. The audience includes those without political or economic influence and who were heavily taxed. Jesus said, "Whoever compels you to go one mile, go with him two." Matthew 5:41 Jesus' message is still relevant today that the pendulum of God's justice is without haste or delay, and actions should communicate social justice much more loudly than words.

With his "Theology of Friendship," Dietrich Bonhoeffer, a German Protestant theologian, embraced what might be considered an extension of Liberation Theology. He believed that "to love one's neighbor is to enter into the life of the other and accept some responsibility for the neighbor's history."[75]

One such example was Bonhoeffer's friendship with Franklin Fisher, an African American student from Birmingham, Alabama, with whom he became acquainted while Fisher was teaching at Union Theological Seminary. Fisher did his fieldwork at the Abyssinian Baptist Church, located in New York City. During the assignment, he introduced Bonhoeffer to spirituals, and he gained an appreciation for this music genre. Through his friendship with Fisher and his firsthand observations of the many injustices encountered by African Americans, Bonhoeffer more fully embraced the concept of God's compassion toward the oppressed. Subsequently, "he became a smart and sensitive critic of American racism, and this attention to racism seemed to deepen his critiques of German anti-Semitism.[76]

Unfortunately, Bonhoeffer was imprisoned and executed for his theological ideas, which ultimately led him to oppose the Nazi government's anti-Semitic actions. In his classic book, *The Cost of Discipleship*, he penned his own reality with conviction, stating: "When Christ calls a man, he bids him come and die." Likewise, for a worthy cause, all are challenged to take up the cross and follow Christ, whatever the cost of discipleship.

South African apartheid is one powerful example. During my visit to the country, as apartheid was ending in the early 1990s, I observed a great sense of expectation in the atmosphere. The message was the same—the need for a new South Africa where people could peacefully live and work together in brotherly love. Former president of South Africa, Nelson Mandela, was sentenced to Robben Island, a then maximum-security prison for the enemies of apartheid, for

---

75 https://politicaltheology.com/bonhoeffer-and-the-politics-of-friendship/
76 https://politicaltheology.com/bonhoeffer-and-the-politics-of-friendship/

nearly three decades, a reminder of what undaunting courage for a worthy cause looks like when the pursuit of social justice refuses to be silent.

JUSTICE IS BLIND

It is essential for those empowered to facilitate justice to remember that "Lady Justice" wears a blindfold, a symbol of fairness and equal justice. Yet, there are notable injustices against African Americans and other minorities. Far too many deaths of African Americans have resulted from encounters with law enforcement officers. While African Americans "account for less than 13 percent of the U.S. population, they are killed by police at more than twice the rate of White Americans. An overwhelming majority of people shot and killed by police are male — over 95 percent. More than half the victims are between twenty and forty years old."[77]

It should come as no surprise that young African American males experience anxiety when pulled over in traffic or approached by a policeman.

These daunting statistics should urge the United States Department of Justice to mandate proper training and education of law enforcement officers sworn to protect American citizens, emphasizing fairness, impartiality, and honesty. Parents are equally responsible for educating children from an early age to respect law enforcement with a disposition of respect and peaceful cooperation. To reverse the deadly trend of police killings, all parties should find ways to build trust and mutual respect. Clergy and churches can also play a significant role by teaching spiritual, moral, and ethical principles to contribute to a civil and peaceful society.

OVERCROWDED PRISONS

Prisons in America are dangerously overcrowded and with a disproportionate rate of African American males. In many cases, they received stiffer sentencing, following the guidelines of The Violent Crime Control and Law Enforcement Act of 1994, commonly referred to as the 1994 Crime Bill. Its three-strikes provision has meant life in prison for many African Americans. Former President William J. Clinton initiated the legislation and "Expressed regret over the portions of the measure that led to increased prison population like the three-strikes provision."[78] The "Three-Strikes" laws allow prosecutors to seek

---

77 https://www.washingtonpost.com/graphics/investigations/police-shootings-database/

78 Kasie (October 8, 2014). "Bill Clinton: Prison sentences to take center stage in 2016". MSNBC. Retrieved June 2, 2015.

harsher sentences for lesser crimes."[79]

The Southern Poverty Law Center's Three Strikes Project has successfully assisted nonviolent offenders' move from prison to parole. Such as in the case of Fair Wayne Bryant, who received a life sentence in Louisiana State prison for attempting to steal hedge clippers. After serving twenty-four years, he was now free. Nicky Patterson is another example. He earned a basketball scholarship to college, but after becoming a father, he dropped out of college to provide for his family and sold marijuana and cocaine. Because he had two prior convictions, he was sentenced to 26 years in the Mississippi State prison when convicted on the third charge of drug possession. The Southern Poverty Law Center (SPLC) assisted him with going from prison to parole, and, according to Jade Morgan, the SPLC attorney who represented Patterson, "the Three Strikes Law' does not reduce crime rates or promote deterrence."[80]

On the contrary, some elected government officials believe that longer sentences prevent crime and propose privatizing and building more prisons. The social inequalities that contribute to mass incarceration represent an economic boost to some areas. According to the Bureau of Justice Statistics, the annual cost of "Mass incarceration in the United States is $81 billion."[81]

Mass imprisonment is a bandage on a much bigger issue or another form of treating the symptoms without addressing the monumental recidivism problem. Breaking the cycle of repeated criminal behavior should be the goal, and it will potentially offer relief to taxpayers. The volume cost to incarcerate an inmate FY 2018 was $37,449.00 ($102.60 per day), according to the Federal Prisons Bureau (11/19/2019).[82]

Interestingly, college tuition costs are comparable, with an average of $36,880 for private colleges, $10,440 at public colleges (in-state residents), and $26,820 at public colleges (out-of-state residents).[83] The best option from now on is to invest in the future of African Americans during adolescence and

---

79 October 19, 2020, *Washington Post*

80 https://www.splcenter.org/news/2020/03/17/splcs-three-strikes-project-helps-nonviolent-offenders-move-prison-parole

81 https://eji.org/news/mass-incarceration-costs-182-billion-annually/

82 https://www.federalregister.gov/documents/2019/11/19/2019-24942/annual-determination-of-average-cost-of-incarceration-fee-coif

83 https://www.collegedata.com/en/pay-your-way/college-sticker-shock/how-much-does-college-cost/whats-the-price-tag-for-a-college-education/#:~:text=In%202

prepare them for college through mentoring programs and math and reading camps.

There are many hypotheses for the disproportionate number of African Americans in prison, including racial profiling. "Nearly 50,000 legal restrictions against people with arrest and conviction records routinely block access to jobs, housing, and educational opportunities, which significantly contributes towards high rates of increased interactions with the criminal justice system and re-incarceration of people who have been released from prison. Further, nearly 75% of formerly incarcerated people are still unemployed a year after release. A lack of stable employment increases the likelihood that an individual will return to jail or prison. In fact, research has found that joblessness is the single most important predictor of recidivism."[84]

I have personally experienced profiling more than once, too: having been asked for additional identification at banks, denied check cashing privileges, monitored by a retail salesperson, ignored by taxi drivers, and stopped by police for no apparent reason. One memorable incident was during a move from Alabama to Tennessee in a medium-sized U-Haul truck. Careful to adhere to all traffic laws, I deliberately drove slightly under the speed limit and made sure I followed all other traffic rules. Still, the blue lights signaled for me to stop as I entered a West Tennessee town. Ten minutes later, I responded to a query of who, what, when, and where questions related to me personally and the U-Haul truck, with no mention of any violation. Fortunately, the encounter ended peacefully.

We need to give credit to police departments that have attempted to address racial profiling by enforcing existing policies and regulations, providing training, and monitoring police officers' field activities. All such efforts are commendable but have not sufficiently addressed the colossal racial profiling or overcrowded prison issues. As a nation, by creating opportunities and access to technology, healthcare, education, and poverty in America, we must identify and address the root causes of these inequities.

FIRST STEP ACT- CRIMINAL JUSTICE BILL

The First Step Act was drafted to address federal sentencing reform, reduce recidivism, initiate programs and activities to improve prison outcomes and assist with transitions from federal prisons. Former White House senior adviser and son-in-law of former President Donald Trump, Jared Kushner, spearheaded

---

84 https://www.naacp.org/criminal-justice-fact-sheet/

the First Step Act. Kushner's father, Charles Kushner, was "Convicted in 2005 for preparing false tax returns, witness retaliation, and making false statements to the Federal Election Commission."[85] He pleaded guilty and was sentenced to two years in prison, serving 14 months at a federal prison camp in Montgomery, Alabama. Charles Kushner completed the remainder of his sentence in a halfway house in Newark, New Jersey. This experience influenced Jared Kushner to explore the potential reformation of the federal criminal justice system, suggesting that "For all those who are deserving of a second chance, this legislation [First Step Act] will make a meaningful and measurable difference in their lives."[86]

Kushner encountered pushback from some members of congress as they felt the First Act Bill did not go far enough in achieving sentencing reform and reduction of the prison population. This was voiced by "More than 100 civil rights groups who opposed the bill, arguing that the votes were there for sentencing reform."[87]

Former Attorney General Jefferson Sessions, who said to Kushner" "If the boy does the crime, you've got to lock him up," was required to do the following:[88] "Assess the Federal Bureau of Prisons' existing prisoner risk and needs assessment system; develop and evaluate a new risk and needs assessment system; develop recommendations regarding effective evidence-based recidivism reduction programs and activities; and conduct research and data analysis on evidence-based programs and assessment tools."[89]

Kushner was determined to push through and assembled unlikely allies in support of the First Step Act, which included the Koch brothers, Kim Kardashian West, and Alice Johnson, an advocate for criminal reform who was released from prison after serving twenty-one years of a life sentence for trafficking cocaine. She was an invited guest of former President Donald Trump during his State of the Union address on February 5, 2019; she received a standing ovation.

Unfortunately, the First Step Act only applies to inmates incarcerated in federal prisons, not state prisons and jails where many African Americans are incarcerated. Though modest by some standards, it relaxes the federal three-strikes rule. Additionally, it prohibits the shackling of pregnant women, promotes el-

---

85 https://www.businessinsider.com/trump-pardoned-charles-kushner-jared-father-crimes-2020-12

86 https://www.nytimes.com/2018/12/14/us/politics/jared-kushner-criminal-justice-bill.html

87 https://www.brennancenter.org/our-work/analysis-opinion/how-first-step-act-became-law-and-what-happens-next

88 https://www.cnn.com/2022/07/29/politics/jeff-sessions-jared-kushner-criminal-justice-reform/index.html

89 https://nij.ojp.gov/topics/articles/nijs-role-under-first-step-act

derly release programs, and allows prisoners to complete their sentences in home confinement or halfway houses. There is a need for more educating, counseling, and drug recovery programs, which the First Step Act does not address.

Kushner's efforts were successful as he mobilized bi-partisan support to pass the First Step Act, which former President Donald Trump signed into law on December 21, 2018, during the 115th United States Congress. Kushner's father was later pardoned by Trump "As part of a late-hour clemency spree during the final days of his presidency."[90]

There is an urgent need for criminal justice reform in the nation that will change the outcomes of the lives of many who are incarcerated. This journey will require bipartisan support in Congress and members of the faith community working collaboratively together.

ENVIRONMENTAL SOCIAL JUSTICE

A visible link between the environment and social justice is needed to ensure the equitable distribution of environmental benefits, even as essential as clean water and air. Pollution abatement and landscape improvements would also prove to be most advantageous to minorities, i.e., African Americans, who live in communities where pollutants fill the air. While the United States Environmental Protection Agency (EPA) is responsible for creating standards and laws for protecting the environment for all people, far too many African Americans are subject to environmental injustice. According to the American Lung Association, "African American communities suffered the greater risk of premature death from particle pollution than those who live in communities that are predominately white."[91]

In some instances, and based on income, African Americans are less likely to relocate to the suburbs to experience a better air quality index. Additionally, people who live in urban cities for an extended period experience environmental stress and are more susceptible to asthma and heart and respiratory disease.

Climate change appears to be at the heart of many environmental justice maladies. For example, when fossil fuels such as coal, oil, and natural gas generate energy, they release carbon dioxide, which traps heat, contributing to climate change and global warming. Climate change is subsequently responsible for "More frequent wildfires, longer periods of drought in some regions, and an

---

90 https://abcnews.go.com/Politics/wireStory/kushner-pardon-revives-loathsome-tale-tax-evasion-sex-74891757

91 https://www.lung.org/clean-air/outdoors/who-is-at-risk/disparities

increase in the number, duration, and intensity of tropical storms."[92]

Ultimately, droughts and floods increase food prices as farmers will have to spend more money on irrigation or face the loss of crops due to drought. These conditions circumstantially contribute to food deserts in some urban communities where African Americans reside, with limited access to healthy food or even grocery stores. In some communities, it is easier to purchase fast foods with empty calories than fresh food. Also, when environmental pollutants are unregulated, the chances of water systems becoming vulnerable increase immensely. In most cases, underserved communities are usually at a higher risk of not receiving governmental protection and funding. Such was the case when residents of Flint, MI, discovered potent neurotoxicants contaminating their drinking water with lead. Sadly, "90 people were sickened, and 12 died from exposure to waterborne legionella bacteria."[93]

The story began in 2014 when the city switched its water supply to the Flint River from Lake Huron to cut costs. Corrosive river water caused lead to leak from pipes, contaminating the drinking water and causing an outbreak of Legionnaires' disease. Residents started to complain about the odor, the brown color, and the brackish taste. The city issued a boil water advisory after fecal bacteria were identified in the water.

Flint is 54% African American according to the United States Census, July 2021, and approximately "40% of people live in poverty."[94] Researchers from Cornell and the University of Michigan concluded that the water crisis impacted residents who "suffered a range of adverse physical and mental health symptoms potentially linked to the crisis in the years during and following it, with Black residents affected disproportionately." [95]

While the state government has assured residents that the water is safe to drink, many residents still find it hard to drink the city's water or trust the state government to continue providing funds for the replacement of pipes that could potentially correct the issues associated with the city's water. However, residents applauded a settlement lawsuit that was approved on November 10, 2022, by United States District Judge Judith Levy for $626 million. City contractors also continue to excavate pipes to determine what hidden risks remain.

---

92 https://climate.nasa.gov/effects/

93 https://www.pbs.org/wgbh/frontline/article/flint-water-crisis-deaths-likely-surpass-official-toll/

94 https://www.wwdmag.com/flint-water-crisis/news/10939678/the-flint-water-crisis-7-years-later

95 https://news.cornell.edu/stories/2021/04/water-crisis-took-toll-flint-adults-physical-mental-health

Jackson, Mississippi, was the site of a similar case in August 2022, after the city experienced heavy rains that caused the Pearl River to flood, affecting the pumps at the O B Curtis water treatment plant for the city. Unfortunately, this water crisis was the straw that broke the camel's back, manifested by discolored water coming from the faucets with an odor, visible dirt, and sediments. Citizens were initially required to boil water before drinking; however, it became increasingly impossible to drink, bathe, cook, clean, and prepare infant formula due to the water crisis.Sadly, this incident came as no surprise to city officials, who were aware of operational failures and understaffing at the water treatment plant. President Joseph Biden approved an emergency declaration over the water crisis in the State of Mississippi and ordered Federal assistance.

Jackson's population is approximately 149,000, with 82% comprising African Americans. During the crisis and when the water was eventually shut off, many organizations and agencies distributed water to residents. Other residents had to purchase bottled water from neighboring municipalities. However, this became expensive over time for families, especially the elderly and those receiving government assistance, since "The poverty rate in Jackson is 28.9%. One out of every 3.5 residents of Jackson lives in poverty."[96]

The water crisis resulted in health challenges as residents were exposed to dangerously high concentrations of lead and E. coli. Others experienced dehydration, malnutrition, hair loss, skin rashes, and digestive issues. However, the water crisis in Jackson, according to Richard Mizelle Jr., a historian of medicine at the University of Houston, "Is a window into that neglect that many people have experienced for much of their lives."[97]

The infrastructure decline resulted from insufficient funds from the state government over many years due to demographic changes that adversely impacted the city's revenue. "Its tax base has eroded the past few decades as the population decreased—the result of mostly white flight to suburbs that began after public schools were integrated in 1970."[98]

The boiling water advisory was eventually lifted; however, "Jackson's water system would cost an estimated $1 billion. And another $1 billion for the sewage system."[99]

---

96 https://www.welfareinfo.org/poverty-rate/mississippi/jackson

97 https://khn.org/news/article/jackson-mississippi-bottled-water-crisis/

98 *USA TODAY* August 31, 2022

99 https://www.clarionledger.com/story/news/local/2022/08/30/jackson-mississippi-ongoing-water-crisis/65464315007/

The torrential rains and flooding resulted from climate change, and those most at risk are members of society who are vulnerable.

The Bible supports the belief that humans are stewards of God's creation, which includes the responsibility of preserving the environment by making wise choices. Webster's dictionary defines stewardship as "Careful and responsible management of something entrusted to one's care." Mismanagement of the environment is often guided by our lifestyle and preference, resulting in climate change, species extinction, rising sea levels, and shrinking mountain glaciers. We can choose to move forward by taking the appropriate actions or lamenting over the decline of the environment in despair. All people, especially Christians, should be motivated by Scripture to be responsible stewards. Many biblical passages support this position.

"Then God said, 'Let Us make man in Our image, according to Our likeness; let them have dominion over the fish of the sea, over the birds of the air, and over the cattle, over all the earth and over every creeping thing that creeps on the earth.'" (Genesis 1:26).

"Then God blessed them, and God said to them, "Be fruitful and multiply; fill the earth and subdue it; have dominion over the fish of the sea, over the birds of the air, and over every living thing that moves on the earth." (Genesis 1:28).

"Then the Lord God took the man and put him in the garden of Eden to tend and keep it." (Genesis 2:15).

"Therefore do not defile the land which you inhabit, in the midst of which I dwell; for I the Lord dwell among the children of Israel." (Numbers 35:34).

"The earth is the Lord's, and all its fullness, The world and those who dwell therein. For He has founded it upon the seas, And established it upon the waters" (Psalm 24:1-2).

In anticipation of the Second Coming of Jesus Christ, when "The elements will melt with fervent heat" (2 Peter 3:10), it is important to continue to preserve the environment to the extent possible. Remarkably, Christ will create a new heaven and earth at His second return (Isaiah 65:17; Revelation 21:1), which will end environmental issues forever.

This nation must take the leadership role in addressing climate change globally. Below is the ranking of the top 10 carbon dioxide producing nations:
• China, with more than 10,065 million tons of CO2 released

- United States, with 5,416 million tons of CO2

- India, with 2,654 million tons of CO2

- Russia, with 1,711 million tons of CO2

- Japan, 1,162 million tons of CO2

- Germany, 759 million tons of CO2

- Iran, 720 million tons of CO2

- South Korea, 659 million tons of CO2

- Saudi Arabia, 621 million tons of CO2

- Indonesia, 615 million tons of CO2[100]

It will require each of these nations taking a responsible effort to reduce carbon dioxide emissions. An ideal goal would be 100% clean energy and net-zero emissions, all through greener living. Green living includes:

- Renewable energy.

- Eco-friendly technology.

- Recyclable materials.

- Eco-friendly cleaning products.

- Planting trees helps remove carbon dioxide from the air.

Just as America could put a man on the moon, we can resolve the climate issue. Future generations stand to benefit immensely. Climate change is a human-made threat to our planet and a global issue that is polarizing, as "About 97% of climate scientists have concluded that human-caused climate change is happening."[101]

THE INFLATION REDUCTION ACT

Some remarkable progress toward improving climate change took place when President Joseph Biden signed into law, The Inflation Reduction Act during the 117th United States Congress on August 16, 2022. The historic legislation addressed climate solutions and environmental justice. The Bill authorized

---

100 https://climatetrade.com/which-countries-are-the-worlds-biggest-carbon-polluters/

101 https://climate.nasa.gov/scientific-consensus/

$369 billion in spending on energy and climate change. It is expected to reduce "Greenhouse gas emissions to 40% below 2005 levels by 2030." https://www.energy.gov/articles/doe-projects-monumental-emissions-reduction-inflation-reduction-act, Theclimate and energy provision will additionally include "Tax credits for households to offset energy costs, investments in clean energy production and tax credits aimed at reducing carbon emissions."[102]

Other provisions in the Bill included: "Cutting prescription drug cost, lowering health care costs, and reducing the deficit." The White House Briefing Room August 15, 2022, The Inflation Reduction Act is still in its infancy, but history and the environment will confirm its success.

REFLECTING MORE ON THE TOPIC:

What were your most meaningful takeaways from this chapter?

____

____

____

____

What will you do differently because of your increased awareness?

____

____

____

____

What resources or support do you need to ensure the successful achievement of your goals?

____

____

____

____

---

[102] https://www.forbes.com/advisor/personal-finance/inflation-reduction-act/

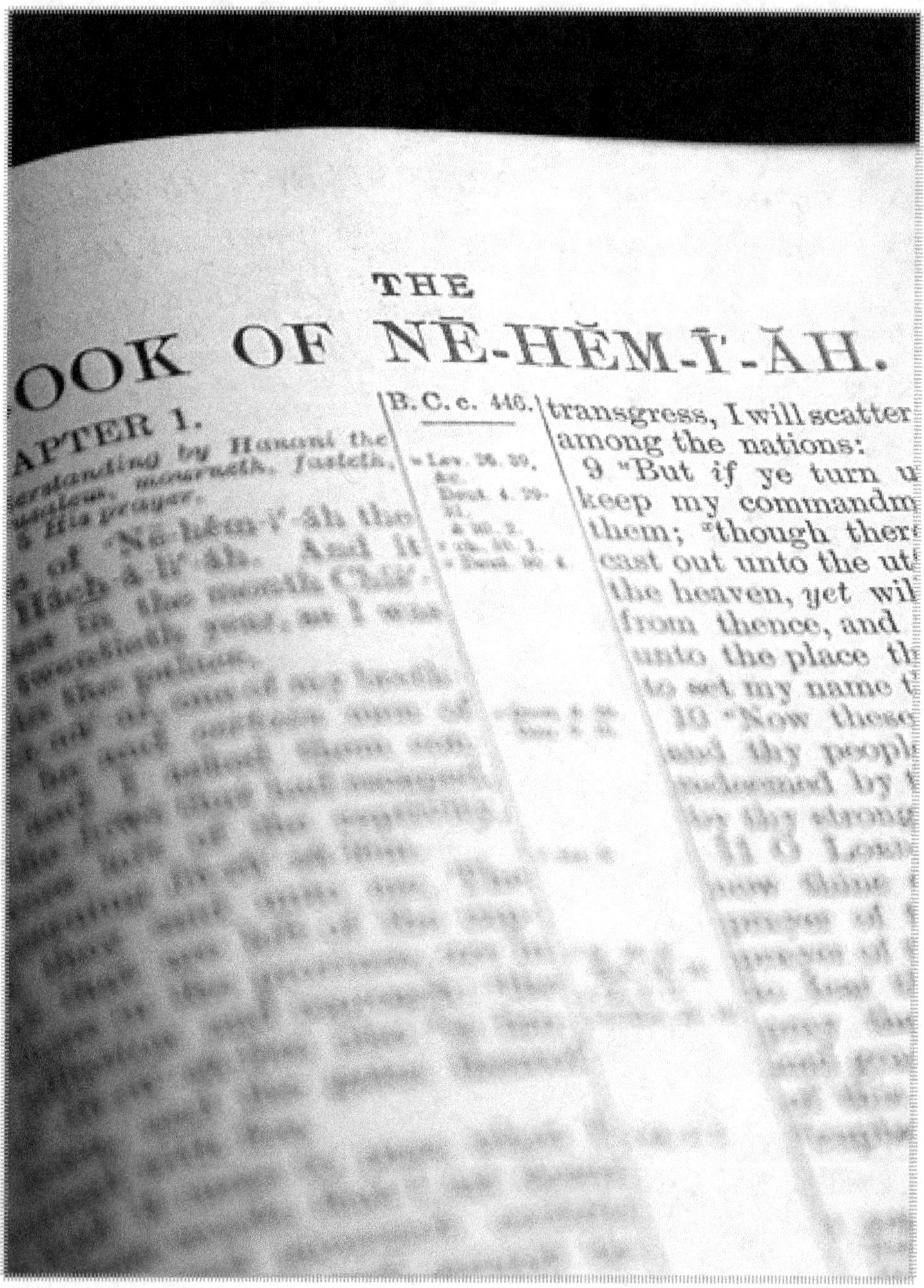
THE
OOK OF NĒ-HĔM-Ĭ-ĂH.
APTER 1.
B.C. c. 446.
transgress, I will scatter
among the nations:
9 "But if ye turn u
keep my commandm
them; "though ther
cast out unto the ut
the heaven, yet wil
from thence, and
unto the place th
to set my name t
10 "Now these
and thy peopl
redeemed by t
by thy strong

CHAPTER 5

BECOME A CHANGE AGENT

We see the problem. The question is, How do we solve it? Of course, that's the million-dollar question. Only when Jesus returns, and there's a new heaven and a new earth, will we have a utopia. But that does not mean we cannot strive to make things better now, even in our sin-ravaged world. What follows are some of my humble suggestions about what we, one by one, can do to make our little corner of the vineyard a better place. First, we must confront the challenging questions of racism, which still plagues America. We need to change, and for the better, too.

LET'S BEGIN RIGHT NOW.

Change seems to be the only steady constant. Seasons, the weather, physiological changes due to aging, technology, relationships, jobs, socio-economic status, and much more comprise change, both anticipated and unanticipated. For example, in my middle school years, I noticed a sudden cracking and deepening in my voice—to the point of embarrassment. The physiological changes involved an increase in my larynx and a lengthening of my vocal cords. It should not have come as a surprise that I was going through puberty, yet I was unprepared for this normal development phase. On another occasion I was singing tenor in the school's choir at the start of the school year I was aware that my voice was changing and without notice it made a complete change during a live performance noticed by me and others in the choir. I went from tenor to baritone not by choice but due to permanent change. The inevitability of change requires thoughtful preparation for both the challenges and victories that it potentially breeds.

Life, in general, consists of events from birth to death that include physical, emotional, social, and spiritual changes. Seasons of change can also depict some of life's transitions. The unexpected death of my two siblings in 2015, over 45 days, was a season that I hoped was a dream. It was not. This devastating change has changed my family permanently.

On the other hand, there are seasons of change that are so desirable that you want them to endure. For example, the annual family Christmas vacations on the Gulf Coast created some of the most enjoyable times but never seemed enduring enough—as each day brought this welcomed season of change closer to its end.

Solomon eloquently wrote about seasons of change in the book of Ecclesiastes—known in the Hebrew Scriptures as *Qoheleth*, meaning a person who is qualified to address a public assembly. This book is central to understanding the cycles of life, and Solomon, in his wisdom, explains that there is a time for every matter in life. He illustrates this truth by juxtaposing opposites to demonstrate that every cycle in life is essential to one's growth and development. Thus, although a season may not always be a comfortable or convenient time in life, still God, in His providence, has a divine purpose for every life change.

A time for every purpose under heaven:

"A good name is better than precious ointment, And the day of death than the day of one's birth" (Ecclesiastes 7:1).

"The race is not to the swift, Nor the battle to the strong, Nor bread to the wise, Nor riches to men of understanding, Nor favor to men of skill; But time and chance happen to them all." (Ecclesiastes 9:11).

"I have seen servants on horses, While princes walk on the ground like servants." (Ecclesiastes 10:1).

Remember now your Creator in the days of your youth, Before the difficult days come, And the years draw near when you say, "I have no pleasure in them." (Ecclesiastes 12:1).

"Let us hear the conclusion of the whole matter: Fear God, and keep his commandments: for this is the whole duty of man." (Ecclesiastes 12:13).

RESISTANCE TO CHANGE

Despite the inevitability of change, many resist it. People resist change for different reasons, i.e., feeling overwhelmed or stressed, mistrust of leadership, job security, change in routine, and fear of the unknown. In contrast, others do not resist change and are not afraid to enter unchartered areas, even where visible opposition exists. They know how to turn lemons into lemonade and see a half-full glass rather than half empty with the lens of optimism. However, ignoring resistance and expecting it to go away on its own is not wise and, in some cases, can worsen the change process.

It is crucial to address opposition to change, ideally, in a systematic manner. One approach that has worked for me over the years has included these steps:

• Promptly acknowledge and identify the opposition.

• Objectively evaluate the reason for the opposition and be amenable to change.

• Avoid fighting the resistance to minimize its escalation.

• Approach opposition in a spiritual and professional manner.

While leading a small congregation early in my pastoral ministry, I showed up for worship where yellow tape wholly wrapped around the front door of the building and a placard that read, "Condemned by the City of ________." This sudden change came not only as a surprise to me, the pastor but to my parishioners as well.

The question of the moment was, "What do we do now?" Though earlier conversations about renovating had occurred, many members felt it was impossible due to limited financial resources. Others wanted to disband and join with the other congregation in the district. Many others said that no bank would approve the sizable loan needed for renovations due to the small size of the church. Unfortunately, the worship facility had gradually declined over the years due to lack of funds and inadequate building maintenance.

The immediate response was to transition to worship in my home. Unfortunately, members became very comfortable with the house worship and, over time, also became seemingly uninterested in remodeling the church. The result? No progress toward a much-needed change. More than half the members maintained that it just could not be done, and they said so publicly. It was time to acknowledge and identify the opposition. Understanding the reason for the opposition gives one insight. I began showing members the importance of imagining ways to finance the project. Overt naysayers continued to resist and sought to rally support from others. We had more meetings where I sought to encourage people to exercise the faith upon which our denominational beliefs stand. Over the years, I have faced opposition from strong to mild and learned that tough skin is an asset, but much more important is fervent prayer, effective communication and reflective listening.

Eventually, the congregation voted unanimously to move forward with the remodeling project. As a result, the church was completely remodeled without a bank loan and rededicated with the very fitting theme: "With God, all things are Possible."

CHARACTERISTICS OF CHANGE AGENTS

Those open to change, whom I will refer to as "change agents," possess the knowledge, skills, and abilities to inspire generations of people, nations, and governments toward change. These people are persistent, creative, affirming, genuinely concerned about others, and hold both themselves and others accountable for behaving ethically. But unfortunately, they experienced failures and, in some cases, died before realizing the desired change, such as Abraham Lincoln, a true frontiersman, born in a log cabin in Kentucky and yet who became the 16th President of the United States. He successfully presided over a nation at war against itself. Lincoln, who was previously a candidate for the United States Senate, running against Democrat Stephen A. Douglas, quoted Scripture from Mark 3:25 and Matthew 12:25: "A house divided against itself cannot stand."[103]

"The metaphor of a house emphasizes interdependence, cooperation, and shared purpose. It asks how citizens might build and maintain something together, despite natural differences, rather than life and work separately."[104]

The Lincoln administration is credited with the signing of the Emancipation Proclamation and ratification of the Thirteenth Amendment—changes he believed were necessary to ensure the end of slavery. The Thirteenth Amendment stated that "Neither slavery nor involuntary servitude, except as a punishment for crime whereof the party shall have been duly convicted, shall exist within the United States, or any place subject to their jurisdiction."[105] Mississippi was the last state to ratify this amendment in 1995 and formalized it in 2013.

Mahatma Gandhi, born in India during colonial rule, became a lawyer who moved to South Africa for 21 years, where he effectively used nonviolent resistance in his pursuit of civil rights. "Gandhi took the religious principle of <u>ahimsa (doing no</u> harm) common to Buddhism, Hinduism, and Jainism and

103 http://www.abrahamlincolnonline.org/lincoln/speeches/house.htm

104 https://theconversation.com/lincolns-house-divided-speech-teaches-important-lessons-about-todays-political-polarization-97841

105 https://constitutioncenter.org/interactive-constitution/amendment/amendment-xiii

turned it into a non-violent tool for mass action. He used it to fight not only colonial rule but social evils such as racial discrimination and untouchability.[106]

Dr. Martin Luther King Jr. was influenced by Gandhi's principle of nonviolence, which was critical during the American Civil Rights movement. Later, Gandhi played a critical role in the successful campaign for India's independence from the British empire. His famous words, "be the change that you wish to see in the world," epitomize one of the best ways of bringing positive change.

Martin Luther King Jr., the son, and grandson of Baptist ministers, successfully organized nonviolent resistance, including the 1955 Montgomery Bus Boycott, against racial inequality. King's emergence as the leader of the boycott in response to the arrest of Rosa Parks, who refused to surrender her bus seat to a white male passenger, violated the sanctions of the segregated Montgomery bus system that required African Americans to be seated in the back of the bus. In 1963, King assisted with organizing the March on Washington, where he gave the electrifying "I Have a Dream" speech. The speech contains the famous words, "I have a dream that my four little children will one day live in a nation where they will not be judged by the color of their skin, but by the content of their character."[107]

King's diligent work culminated with the 1968 sanitation worker's strike for economic justice in Memphis, Tennessee, where African American sanitation workers, many earning as little as 65 cents an hour, took a nonviolent stance for higher wages. Memphis was also the setting for his famous "I've been to the Mountaintop" speech given one day before his assassination. The closing lines of the address seemed fearlessly predictive of his death yet hope-laden for a much brighter day: I'm not worried about anything. I'm not fearing any man! Mine eyes have seen the glory of the coming of the Lord![108]

King received the Nobel Peace Prize for courageously combating racial inequality through nonviolent resistance. Dr. King's change agent legacy and dream live on in immortality.

CHANGE AGENTS CHOSEN AND LED BY GOD

The Bible, perhaps, provides the most extensive record of change agents. Joseph, who was sold as a slave by his brothers, later became the Governor of

106 http://www.bbc.co.uk/ethics/war/against/nonviolence.shtml

107 https://www.americanrhetoric.com/speeches/mlkihaveadream.htm

108 https://www.americanrhetoric.com/speeches/mlkivebeentothemountaintop.htm

Egypt. By God's design, his journey through slavery, prison, and ultimately the royal courts of Pharaoh results in the sustainment of his family and the entire Jewish nation during a famine. (Genesis 41:37-39)

Moses, an Israelite by birth and the Egyptian Pharaoh's adopted grandson, was chosen by God to liberate the Israelites from slavery. Known as one of the meekest men on earth (Numbers 12:3), he had to unlearn much of what he had been taught 40 years earlier in Egypt to remove barriers to his work as an agent of change. The leadership mantle that he humbly received during his encounter with God at the burning bush proved to be both rewarding and challenging but ultimately resulted in one of the most notable changes in human history. (Exodus 3:1-5).

Daniel's captive service in the royal courts of Babylon—results in his becoming a prominent leader and agent of far-reaching and impactful change within the Babylonian province. His interpretation of Babylonian King Nebuchadnezzar's dreams on two occasions (Daniel 2 and 4) would have both personal and prophetic implications that would transcend the annuls of history to the end of time.

Each of these well-known change agents faced enormous challenges, some even life-threatening, but the noted opposition seemingly set the stage for a divine appointment. Remember, not everyone will accept what you are attempting to do. Nevertheless, they are fine examples of what happens when change agents press forward despite opposition and are unyielding in goal achievement.

JESUS, THE GREATEST CHANGE AGENT

By far, the most miraculous change ever encountered by humanity, salvation unto eternal life, has been wrought by Jesus, the world's Greatest Change Agent (Acts 4:12; Acts 16:31; John 5:24; John 10:28-30). So, who was this incomparable Agent of Change? Christology, the study of Jesus' humanity and divinity, explores the connection between these two aspects of salvation. The incarnation of Jesus is an essential and core doctrine of the Christian Church, which embraces the belief that God became flesh, assumed human nature, and became a man in the form of Jesus, the Son of God and the second person of the Godhead. Twenty centuries later, the doctrine of the incarnation of Jesus is still inconceivable, miraculous, and supernatural. The apostle Paul wrote of the incarnation: "And without controversy great is the mystery of godliness: God was manifest in the flesh, justified in the Spirit, seen of angels, preached unto the Gentiles, believed on in the world, received up into glory." (I Timothy 3:16).

The God of all creation arrived from heaven on a mission to redeem man from the penalty of sin and to restore the fractured relationship between God and man—a needed change (to say the least!). The plan of redemption required the death of one equal to God, so Jesus volunteered to die for the sins of the world—a mystery to both men and angels. His earthly mission begins with His birth, which was predicted in the Old Testament and fulfilled in the New Testament. St. Paul said, "But when the fullness of the time had come, God sent forth His Son, born of a woman, born under the law." Galatians 4:4 Jesus, the Son of God, entered human history as a baby in Bethlehem to make positive changes to the fullest extent possible. The Bible gives us an account of who He is in both the Old and New Testaments:

GOD WITH US

"Therefore, the Lord Himself will give you a sign: Behold, the virgin shall conceive and bear a Son, and shall call His name Immanuel." (Isaiah 7:14).

"Behold, the virgin shall be with child, and bear a Son, and they shall call His name Immanuel," which means "God with us." (Matthew 1:23).

BORN IN BETHLEHEM

"But you, Bethlehem Ephrathah, Though you are little among the thousands of Judah, Yet out of you shall come forth to Me The One to be Ruler in Israel, Whose goings forth are from of old, From everlasting." (Micah 5:2).

"But you, Bethlehem, in the land of Judah, Are not the least among the rulers of Judah; For out of you shall come a Ruler Who will shepherd My people Israel." (Matthew 2:6).

PREPARATION FOR HIS ARRIVAL

"The voice of one crying in the wilderness: "Prepare the way of the Lord; Make straight in the desert A highway for our God. Every valley shall be exalted, And every mountain and hill brought low; The crooked places shall be made straight And the rough places smooth." (Isaiah 40:3-4).

"John replied in the words of Isaiah the prophet, "I am the voice of one calling in the wilderness, 'Make straight the way for the Lord." (John 1:23).

LIFE-THREATENING CHANGE AGENT WORK

Thus says the Lord: "A voice was heard in Ramah, Lamentation and bitter weeping, Rachel weeping for her children, Refusing to be comforted for her children Because they are no more." (Jeremiah 31:15).

"A voice was heard in Ramah, Lamentation, weeping, and great mourning, Rachel weeping for her children, Refusing to be comforted, Because they are no more." (Matthew 2:18).

"When Israel was a child, I loved him, And out of Egypt, I called My son." (Hosea 11:1).

"Out of Egypt, I called My Son." (Matthew 2:15).

TRAINED IN AN UNLIKELY PLACE

"And he came and dwelt in a city called Nazareth, that it might be fulfilled which was spoken by the prophets, "He shall be called a Nazarene." (Matthew 2:23).

"Philip found Nathanael and said, "We have found Him of whom Moses in the law, and also the prophets, wrote—Jesus of Nazareth, the son of Joseph." And Nathanael said to him, "Can anything good come out of Nazareth?" Philip said to him, "Come and see." (John 1:45-46).

CHALLENGED TO THE CORE

I imagine if there had been a birth certificate for Jesus, it would have listed His father, Joseph as a carpenter or laborer and His mother, Mary as a homemaker. According to the caste system in Palestine, at His birth, Jesus' profession is predetermined. As an apprentice under Joseph, normally, there would be limits to Jesus' vertical mobility and where he would live. None of these conditions inhibited His understanding of and commitment to His mission. The visit to Jerusalem with His parents suggests that, from childhood, Jesus was keenly aware of His mission, as all agents of change should be: "Now so it was that after three days they found Him in the temple, sitting in the midst of the teachers, both listening to them and asking them questions. And all who heard Him were astonished at His understanding and answers." (Luke 2:46-47).

Still, Jesus faces enormous challenges. Religious leaders became jealous of His miracles, knowledge of the Scriptures, and crowds of followers that emptied their synagogues. Their resentment of His role and work manifests itself with attacks on His genealogy, academic transcript, and theological framework. In response, Jesus challenged the bureaucratic nature of the Pharisees, who had empowered themselves to "safeguard" The Law given at Mount Sinai by adding burdensome laws, ceremonies, and rituals. The religious leaders should have been much more aware of who Jesus was and His mission; after all—they had studied prophecies concerning His birth. Blinded by their ambitions for exaltation by a noble king—all contrary to the Prophet Isaiah's writings, which proclaimed the Messiah as one who would be despised and rejected by men: "A Man of sorrows and acquainted with grief. And we hid, as it were, our faces from Him; He was despised, and we did not esteem Him." (Isaiah 53:3).

Jesus exposed the hypocrisy of the Pharisees and remained focused on His mission to bring salvation to all of humanity. At the same time, Satan worked simultaneously through their plans to abort the mission. He succeeded in convincing the religious leaders that the solution was to rid themselves of Jesus by killing Him. The murder of Jesus would also serve as a public reprimand to Jesus' disciples and followers. But the Pharisees did not understand that Jesus came to die and nothing would deter His mission. (Romans 5:8).

GROWTH OF CHRISTIANITY

After Jesus's ascension and shortly following Pentecost in Acts 2, His disciples and those in the upper room received the anointing of the Holy Spirit. They dismissed their ambitions and dedicated their lives to reflect His character and proceeded to carry out the Gospel Commission given in Matthew 28:19-20. Later, St. Paul was converted on the Damascus Road (Acts 9:1-19) and became the catalyst for taking the message of Jesus to Gentiles throughout the Roman Empire. The seven churches in Revelation 1-3 that John wrote about from the Greek Island of Patmos were established by St. Paul's ministry and still serve as an inspiration for the Christian Church today. Jesus' life and ministry inspired and motivated billions of people, even non-Christians, for positive change—impacting multiple aspects of society, including marriage and family, art, music, literature, equality of human beings, and much more. According to the Center for the Study of Global Christianity (CSGC) at Gordon-Conwell Theological Seminary, there are more than 2.6 billion Christians globally. https://goodfaith-media.org/global-christian-population-projected-to-reach-3-3-billion-by-2050/

No other leader has faced such opposition, rejection, remonstrance, harsh criticism, etc., and completed his mission—a genuinely celebratory outcome. Accordingly, the Christian calendar celebrates two significant holidays in honor of the life of Jesus: Christmas, celebrating the birth of Jesus, and Easter, which commemorates His death and resurrection. Both are meaningful in the Christian church, particularly as it relates to salvation. Moreover, Jesus's positive impact on the Christian world 2,000 years later continues to expand the globe.

CHANGE AGENTS BUILD RELATIONSHIPS BEFORE A CRISIS

Change agents know the importance of building bridges and sustainable relationships with key stakeholders well before crises, i.e., police departments and state and local government officials. This outcome is not difficult to accomplish if one is willing to invest time and energy in working with community leaders. The cohesive effect of such relationships breeds both unity and trust: "Great leaders unite, they do not divide, and they always start by building trust, not walls."[109]

While pastoring in Mississippi, I realized that a disproportionate number of African Americans were receiving longer sentences than white offenders—a cycle I desired to see broken. My interest prompted immediate involvement in local civic affairs within my city of residence, which led to an invitation to sit on a committee of elected officials responsible for studying the court system's sentencing guidelines. Fortunately, my well-established relationship with an elected state official contributed to my being on the committee, which was eventually able to recommend changes to sentencing outcomes that were considered for legislation. However, it required significant time commitments for causes that were wellworth it.

While I was pastoring in California, low graduation rates challenged the local school system. The parishioners of our church desired to contribute to a more positive graduation trend. They leveraged an established relationship with a local school administrator to begin an after-school tutoring program for elementary and middle school students, focusing on a more robust subject comprehension, increased confidence, and the development of learning strategies on individualized levels. The program's high level of success resulted in improved grades and high school graduation for participants—contributions from parishioners who were committed to a worthy cause funded the program.

An additional consideration is to be willing to serve voluntarily without expecting pay or anything else in return. Such was my volunteer service as a fire and police department chaplain in two cities, very personally rewarding and allowing me to build relationships with government officials—a sitting and former governor and several members of the state Senates and House. In addition, volunteer service in the community opened doors of opportunities to give the opening invocation for legislative sessions.

However, not everyone will be receptive. While pastoring in Alabama, I sought opportunities to get involved with my community by identifying and

---

109 https://www.forbes.com/sites/worldeconomicforum/2016/05/25/how-to-build-bridges-not-walls-at-work/#283182981000

supporting positive change already in progress and future goals. One of my first visits as a new pastor and recent graduate of the seminary was with the pastor of one of the larger churches in the city. The visit was over in record time when the pastor asked, "What church are you from?" When I shared the name of my church, he responded by saying, "I never heard of that church," and the visit ended shortly after that. I did not allow this to breed despair or discouragement. Instead, I gravitated toward those who were inviting and with whom I shared similar interests and goals. I was fortunate to meet my United States Congressman later with whom I built a good relationship. I also received a call from the congressman's office inviting me to attend the inauguration of the president of the United States, William J. Clinton.

Recognizing that not everyone will be interested in building relationships, I reached out to responsive people. As a result, what follows are some strategies that have proven to be vital in building solid and sustainable relationships with local and state government leaders:

- **Stay focused on your purpose**, ensuring it is inclusive of all people and independent of political affiliations.

- **Exercise patience with community leaders**, as most elected officials and community leaders are busy and may not respond directly or have available staff who will promptly return your telephone calls and emails.

- **Come prepared**. Be punctual and prepare for your appointment. Know something about the elected official's interests and pet peeves; be an active listener and sensitive to the official's time. Outline what you are planning to share and monitor the time of your meeting or presentation. Remember, say more with less!

- **Avoid proselytizing**. Remember, the goal of your visit is not to evangelize but to develop a healthy civic relationship.

- **Be a supportive constituent**. Do not reinvent a program that is already functioning successfully.

- **Build on and maintain the civic relationship**. Ask if regularly scheduled meetings are open to the public and be added to the respective social media network.

- **Invite civic leaders to corporate events**. This type of organizational exposure will help to demonstrate the need for the requested support while strengthening the developing relationship.

- **Be polite, gracious, and courteous**. Employ the highest level of Christian virtues during each visit and a follow-up visit with a letter or email thanking them for their time.

- **Be visible in the community**. Roll up your sleeves and go to work!

LEADING CHANGE

Change agents must have the ability to not only embrace but lead change initiatives. In the words of Albert Einstein, "The measure of intelligence is the ability to change," and when done well, the benefits can be far-reaching. They can include, but are not limited to, a substantial degree of buy-in by organizational members, accelerated and sustained change initiatives, and predictability. John Kotter, a thought leader in business, leadership, and change, proposed eight steps for leading change effectively. The story of the prophet Nehemiah, a dynamic change agent used by God to rebuild the walls of Jerusalem after the Babylonian exile, emulates many of the steps included in Kotter's 8-step process for leading change.[110]

STEP ONE: CREATE A SENSE OF URGENCY

In a change process, a sense of urgency is necessary to help others see the need for change. A bold, aspirational opportunity statement that communicates the importance of acting accomplishes this. Leaders must be uncomfortable with the ills and maladies around them as the catalyst for initiating positive change. When Nehemiah received the report that the walls of Jerusalem needed repair, he was utterly disheartened and immediately driven to fasting and prayer, and ultimately, a request was made to the king for a leave of absence to restore the walls. Others who seemed to be comfortable with the situation prior to Nehemiah communicating the importance of acting with a sense of urgency, now seem ready to move forward. This step in the change process supersedes all others, as it is needed to create the climate for understanding why the change is necessary and to gain support and buy-in from those who will participate in the change process. (Nehemiah 1:3, 2:1-5).

STEP TWO: BUILD A GUIDING COALITION

A volunteer army needs a coalition of influential people—born of its ranks—to guide it, coordinate it, and communicate its activities. Ideally,

---

110 https://www.kotterinc.com/8-steps-process-for-leading-change/Change

coalition members agree on the mission, have shared values and mutual trust, and are committed to the cause. Therefore, Nehemiah solicited the support of trustworthy persons to help complete the task of rebuilding the wall. Nehemiah 2:16-18.

STEP THREE: CREATE A VISION FOR CHANGE

Change agents envision the ideal future state. Without vision, it is difficult to navigate through life. Vision gives meaning, value, and purpose to our lives. Solomon said, "Where there is no revelation, the people cast off restraint." (Proverbs 29:18). Inevitably, this requires varying degrees of change driven by strategic initiatives and the need to improve the status quo. In Nehemiah's case, he was embarrassed by the condition of the walls in Jerusalem. Recognizing the dire need for change, he said in Nehemiah 2:17 (NIV): "Then I said to them, "You see the trouble we are in: Jerusalem lies in ruins, and its gates have been burned with fire. Come, let us rebuild the wall of Jerusalem, and we will no longer be in disgrace." He envisioned the rebuilt walls and restored feelings of pride, dignity, and perhaps honor to God since the city of Jerusalem was where God met His people.

STEP FOUR: ENLIST A VOLUNTEER ARMY

Kotter describes the change as a movement and a journey where people are involved based on their desire. He also suggests that "large-scale change can only occur when massive numbers of people rally around a common opportunity." Buy-in is critical in this phase of change. Nehemiah solicited the help of men willing to be a part of the large-scale change project, acknowledging that the skills and abilities they possessed could contribute to the project's success. Their buy-in was evident in multiple ways, including their willingness to put their own lives at risk as part of the mission. (Nehemiah 4:13-15).

STEP FIVE: ENABLE ACTION BY REMOVING BARRIERS

Kotter suggests that removing barriers, such as inefficient processes and hierarchies, provides the freedom necessary to work across silos and generate real impact. This step is mainly about the empowerment of those committed to the change process. In addition to some of the natural barriers that potentially inhibit change, i.e., insufficient funding and bureaucracies, there is often opposition that comes in varying degrees. For example, Nehemiah faced considerable opposition from within and without his coalition. Thus, while some barriers are movable, there are other times when change agents will need to work around them. When this is the case, as with Nehemiah, it will be essential to focus on the mission, working steadily in the change process until the desired change becomes a reality. (Nehemiah 4 & 5).

STEP SIX: GENERATE SHORT-TERM WINS

In Kotter's words, "Wins are the molecules of results. They must be recognized, collected, and communicated—early and often—to track progress and energize volunteers to persist." Amid opposition and ridicule, Nehemiah acknowledges and reports that half of the wall is complete and that the people had worked enthusiastically to accomplish the work. These quick wins helped to inspire the workers to focus more intently on the goal. (Nehemiah 6:15-16).

STEP SEVEN: SUSTAIN ACCELERATION

When things are moving in the right direction, you must keep them moving. Change agents gain credibility when effective change occurs. It would be best if you kept the momentum. Kotter says, "press harder after the first successes. Be relentless with initiating change after change until the vision is a reality." Such was the case with Nehemiah. Completing the wall in 52 days was a significant accomplishment that could have occurred only with sustained acceleration, commitment, and focus. Every measure of success with rebuilding the wall inspired bolder moves until the walls were complete. (Nehemiah 6:15).

STEP EIGHT: INSTITUTE CHANGE

The needed change during Nehemiah's time was for the people to turn their hearts back to God. Their loss of identity as God's people resulted in the need for widespread change and reformation beyond the restoration of the walls. Nehemiah was keenly aware that if his people had any chance of becoming obedient, holy, and worshipful, major reform would be necessary, and such was the case. His change process ultimately included temple, financial, Sabbath and relationship reforms. Every reform and restoration of the walls conveyed that the people belonged to God, who desired to be in constant fellowship with them and was more than capable of protecting and sustaining them.

Nehemiah's leadership was mostly about change and reformation. Though challenged incessantly, his sense of urgency, the community of committed people, compelling vision, and dependence on God resulted in the best outcome: restoring the people's trust in God. (Nehemiah 13).

REFLECTING MORE ON THE TOPIC:

What were your most meaningful takeaways from this chapter?

____

____

____

____

What will you do differently because of your increased awareness?

____

____

____

____

What resources or support do you need to ensure the successful achievement of your goals?

____

____

____

____

E PLURIBUS
UNUM

CHAPTER 6

"E PLURIBUS UNUM - OUT OF MANY, ONE"

Past and current events suggest the time has come for a long-divided nation to become united and honor the motto of its great American Seal: "E Pluribus Unum:" It means, "Out of Many, One." These words convey the concept of unity in diversity, which is fundamental for the continual health and growth of the nation. Of course, unity in diversity, equity, and inclusion are not the same as conformity. But on the other hand, it does represent a way to expand one's knowledge and worldview with notable elements of mutual respect, acceptance, and the celebration of diversity.

When the founding fathers signed the Declaration of Independence, it was an overt act of treason, punishable by death. Yet, they proceeded because they were dedicated and committed to establishing a new nation that would extend religious freedom, asylum from tyranny, and opportunities to succeed for all people. The new nation's Great Seal, proposed by John Adams, Benjamin Franklin, and Thomas Jefferson in 1776, "E Pluribus Unum," a Latin phrase meaning "Out of Many, One," portrayed a nation where ideas would flow together in a democratic form of government. Today, almost 250 years since the signing of the Declaration of Independence, America still awaits the full realization of the principles embedded in *E Pluribus Unum*. The fact that we are still waiting seems overtly evident with multiple inequities among people of color, particularly in education, housing, income, and life expectancy.

EDUCATION

The Brown v. Board of Education decision ruled that racial segregation in public schools was unconstitutional. However, urban schools, where most students are African Americans, receive less funding than smaller suburban school systems where African Americans are in the minority. "Research shows that compared with white students, black students are more likely to be suspended or expelled, less likely to be placed in gifted programs, and subject to lower expectations from their teachers."[111]

During the COVID-19 pandemic, educational outcomes varied for African American students compared to others, in part because African American parents, primarily due to income, were unable to hire teachers or tutors for their homebound children. Learning pods or pandemic pods," small groups that meet in person to study, were inconceivable. There are other gaps. For example: "One-quarter of black teens said they often or sometimes cannot do homework assignments due to lack of reliable access to a computer or internet connectivity, compared with 13% of white teens."[112]

Past and present economic and social conditions are also at the root of achievement gaps. For example, while living in the Northeast, my son was on his high school's Basketball team, and we could predict the condition of the school's facilities where the games were scheduled based on the assigned school district. Unsurprisingly, school districts comprising many students with lower socio-economic status (SES) most often reflected sub-par facilities.

AFFIRMATIVE ACTION

Affirmative action was initiated to improve equal opportunities for African Americans through education and employment during the American Civil Rights Movement. Affirmative Action is not reverse discrimination, nor does it give preferential treatment to African Americans solely on race. The term Affirmative Action was first used by United States President John F. Kennedy when he issued Executive Order 10925 on March 6, 1961. https://www.thoughtco.com/what-is-affirmative-action-2834562 On September 24, 1965 United States President Lyndon B. Johnson issued Executive Order 11246, which was "A key landmark in a series of federal actions aimed at ending racial, religious and ethnic discrimination, prohibiting employment discrimination based on race." https://www.dol.gov/agencies/ofccp/about/executive-order-11246-history

On June 27, 1969, the late Arthur Fletcher, an African American and Assistant Secretary of Labor for United States President Richard Nixon, "Implemented the nation's first federal affirmative-action program, which required federal contractors to meet specified goals in minority hiring" https://www.seattletimes.

---

[111] https://www.apa.org/monitor/2016/11/cover-inequality-school

[112] https://www.pewresearch.org/fact-tank/2020/03/16/as-schools-close-due-to-the-coronavirus-some-u-s-students-face-a-digital-homework-gap/

com/opinion/remembering-arthur-fletcher-father-of-affirmative-action/ Fletcher is known as the "Father of Affirmative Action."

Despite the progress of the American Civil Rights Movement, on June 29, 2023, the United States Supreme Court decided a landmark case, Students for Fair Admissions v. Harvard, where it was ruled that holding race-conscious college admissions processes is unconstitutional under the 14th Amendment's Equal Protection Clause. The United States Supreme Court ruled that Affirmative Action policies at Harvard and the University of North Carolina that consider a student's race for college admissions are unconstitutional. This ruling does not change the notable reality that African Americans are still underrepresented at top tier colleges and universities. Affirmative Acton allowed institutions to be more intentional in accepting "qualified" African American applicants. According to the American Council on Education, diversity enriches the experience of students at every level. Reportedly, "It promotes personal growth-and a healthy society, It strengthens communities and the workplace and It enhances America's economic competitiveness." https://www.acenet.edu/Documents/BoardDiversityStatement-June2012.pdf However, there are opposing opinions. According to the Pew Research Center, "In a survey conducted in spring 2023, half of U.S. adults said they "disapprove of selective colleges and universities taking race and ethnicity into account in admissions decisions in order to increase racial and ethnic diversity." https://www.pewresearch.org/short-reads/2023/06/16/americans-and-affirmative-action-how-the-public-sees-the-consideration-of-race-in-college-admissions-hiring/

United States Supreme Court Chief Justice, John Roberts, who wrote the decision for the court's majority, stated "The nation's colleges and universities must use colorblind criteria in admissions." https://www.npr.org/2023/06/29/1181138066/affirmative-action-supreme-court-decision Responding in dissent, United States Supreme Court Justice Sonia Sotomayor wrote that the majority opinion would impose a "superficial rule of colorblindness" in a country where race still matters and racial discrimination still exists" https://rollcall.com/2023/06/29/supreme-court-limits-use-of-race-in-college-admissions-decisions/ As a part of this ruling, the United States Supreme Court made exemptions which included service academies continuing race-conscious admissions policies that have been historically justified by the need for diversity in the Commissioned Corps. Also, it should be noted that at the time of this publication, "43% of Harvard's white admits were legacy students, recruited athletes, children of faculty and staff or were applicants affiliated with donors…

70% of Harvard's donor-related or legacy applicants were white." https://www.usatoday.com/story/news/education/2023/07/03/legacy-admissions-complaint-after-affirmative-action-ruling/70380084007/

Ideally, the United States Supreme Court ruling will inspire African American students to give greater consideration to Historically Black Colleges and Universities (HBCUs).

According to Dr. Michael Lomax, President and CEO of the United Negro College Fund (UNCF), HBCUs are more important [now] than ever for these six reasons:

- Outsized Impact, Low-Cost = "Best Buy" in Education

- Meeting the Needs of Low-income, First-generation Students

- Lower Costs Narrow the Racial Wealth Gap

- Campus Climate Fosters Success

- Addresses the Nation's Under- and Unemployment Crisis

- HBCUs Offer a True Value/Values Proposition

https://medium.com/@DrMichaelLomax/6-reasons-hbcus-are-more-important-than-ever-6572fc27c715#.wtmfraof6

As a graduate of an HBCU, there is an acknowledgement of the importance of the value-added and transformative experience one can potentially encounter by learning in an environment that fosters nurturing, a sense of belonging, promotion of confidence, self-esteem, and shared goals for success.

HOUSING

Housing inequality is widening for African Americans; they are disproportionately failing to qualify for loans. "Black applicants are twice as likely to be denied for a mortgage compared to their White counterparts". https://www.nar.realtor/blogs/economists-outlook/racial-disparities-in-homeownership-rates The starting point for homeownership is typically generational wealth, which passes from one generation to the next. Homeownership is almost impossible to achieve when "At just 41.7 percent, Black households have the lowest homeownership rate nationally—30.0 percentage points lower than white households." https://www.jchs.harvard.edu/blog/nearly-every-state-people-color-are-less-likely-own-homes-compared-white-households In some instances, real estate agents are apprehensive about African American clients because they question whether they can qualify for a loan. While in ministry in the Bay Area, where the housing price is above the national average in the United States, I recall touring a home that seemed perfect for our family of three. When we expressed interest in the house, the professionally dressed and polite agent's next question was, "Can you afford a house in this range?" We knew, with certainty, that the agent was judging us by the color of our skin.

INCOME

The wealth of African Americans and whites continue to widen as the result of "Accumulated inequality and discrimination, as well as differences in power and opportunity that can be traced back to this nation's inception."[113] The median income for Black households in 2021 " Was $48,297, according to the U.S. Census Bureau. That's compared with $74,262 for white households — a difference of $25,965, or 35%." https://www.lendingtree.com/debt-consolidation/black-and-white-disparities-study/#:~:text=2021%3A%20The%20median%20income%20for,of%20%2425%2C965%2C%20or%2035%25.

"The median Black household in America has around $24,000 in savings, investments, home equity, and other elements of wealth. The median White household: around $189,000, a disparity that has worsened in recent decades." https://www.rand.org/blog/rand-review/2023/05/what-would-it-take-to-close-americas-black-white-wealth-gap.html This data helps to explain the reason many African American families do not take yearly vacations, own businesses, and must borrow to finance their children's education. Without a doubt, education is vital in achieving a higher income bracket, but for African Americans, that is not always the case. "Even black workers with an advanced degree experience a significant wage gap compared with their white counterparts."[114]

LIFE EXPECTANCY

African Americans' life expectancy is lower than most other ethnic groups: "Provisional data from 2021 show that overall life expectancy across all racial/ethnic groups was 76.1 years. Life expectancy for Black people was only 70.8 years compared to 76.4 years for White people and 77.7 years for Hispanic people." https://www.kff.org/racial-equity-and-health-policy/report/key-data-on-health-and-health-care-by-race-and-ethnicity/#:~:text=Provisional%20data%20from%202021%20show,77.7%20years%20for%20Hispanic%20people. Many contributing factors are responsible for decreasing life expectancy for African Americans, including "heart disease, stroke, cancer, asthma, influenza and pneu-

---

113 https://www.brookings.edu/blog/up-front/2020/02/27/examining-the-black-white-wealth-gap/

114 https://www.epi.org/blog/black-white-wage-gaps-are-worse-today-than-in-2000/

monia, diabetes, HIV/AIDS, and homicide."[115]

African American males have the lowest life expectancy of any ethnic group in the United States. Some of the contributing factors are hypertension, kidney disease, obesity, and strokes. Additionally, "life expectancy and other health outcomes are affected by exposures to a wide range of social, economic, and biological risk factors during critical periods of the life course."[116]

African American males are, in most cases, the most vulnerable to stress-related conditions. According to the Centers for Disease Control and Prevention, "Discrimination, which includes racism, can lead to chronic and toxic stress and shapes social and economic factors that put some people from racial and ethnic minority groups at increased risk for COVID-19."[117] There are other stressors that African Americans encounter that contribute to short life expectancy—and discrimination is on this list. "Many studies have documented that various forms of racism and discrimination influence mental health and well-being.[118]

Further, during the COVID-19 pandemic, because of pre-existing conditions and health disparities, African Americans were at a higher risk of contracting COVID-19 and "much more likely than white people to die from the virus."[119]

President Joseph Biden aggressively instituted many initiatives designed to educate Americans regarding the importance of getting vaccinated, ensuring the availability of all approved COVID-19 vaccines to every citizen. Interestingly, African Americans, who were disproportionately represented among those who contracted and/or died from COVID-19, represented one of the lowest percentages among ethnic groups receiving at least one dose of the vaccine according to the CDC and at the time of this publication.[120]

Some possible reasons could include challenges associated with accessing information about vaccine availability and registration, which was primarily online, as well as some agencies' mismanagement of programs intended to make the vaccine available in communities of color. Then there is the issue of mistrust.

115 https://minorityhealth.hhs.gov/omh/browse.aspx?lvl=3&lvlid=61

116 https://www.ncbi.nlm.nih.gov/pmc/articles/PMC4984780/

117 https://www.cdc.gov/coronavirus/2019-ncov/community/health-equity/race-ethnicity.html

118 https://www.ncbi.nlm.nih.gov/pmc/articles/PMC3783344/

119 https://www.pewtrusts.org/en/research-and-analysis/blogs/stateline/2020/05/27/covid-19-is-crushing-black-communities-some-states-are-paying-attention

120 https://www.cdc.gov/mmwr/volumes/70/wr/mm7005e1.htm?s_cid=mm7005e1_w

Most notably, the lingering history of the Tuskegee Syphilis Study by the United States Department of Health and the Centers for Disease Control and Prevention in Tuskegee, AL, has likely contributed to the potential skepticism about the vaccine. African American males were initially told that the treatment was free and that the study would last six months, which turned into forty years."[121]

The study was a retrospective study of untreated syphilis, and those infected did not receive the penicillin vaccination, which was the standard treatment for syphilis. As a result, "28 patients died directly from syphilis, 100 died from complications related to syphilis, 40 of the patients' wives were infected with syphilis, and 19 children were born with congenital syphilis." Kim, Oliver J.; Magner, Lois N. (2018). *A History of Medicine*. Page 138.

The Tuskegee Study joins other instances that have contributed to a legacy of mistrust among African Americans, where gross violations of bioethics occurred, such as the story of Henrietta Lacks who died of cervical cancer in 1951. Samples of her cells were harvested without Lack's knowledge as they became known as HeLa cells, resulting in groundbreaking medical research which included "The polio vaccine and contributed to advancements in cancer, AIDS and Parkinson's treatments and the development of the recent coronavirus vaccines. In total it's estimated that HeLa cells have saved over 10 million lives." https://www.alamedahealthsystem.org/henrietta-lacks/#:~:text=In%20addition%20to%20HPV%2C%20the,saved%20over%2010%20million%20lives.[122]

This makes it critical for the United States government to build bridges that will help to create trusting relationships with African American citizens, especially with regard to government-sponsored medical assistance. Significantly improved health and increased longevity just might result from the same.

CONTROVERSIAL AND CONTRADICTORY SYMBOLISM

Much of the symbolism designed to portray American heritage, legacies, and ideals have historically fallen short of intended implications and even led to a degree of controversy and discord. The Confederate Flag, statues of Confederate leaders, and military base names are among some of the most controversial symbols.

REDESIGNATION OF UNITED STATES MILITARY BASES

The earliest United States military criteria for naming a post or fort is documented in The War Department General Order Number 11, dated 8 February

---

121 https://www.history.com/news/the-infamous-40-year-tuskegee-study

122 https://www.blackpast.org/african-american-history/henrietta-lacks-and-debate-over-ethics-bio-medical-research/

1832. The responsibility rested entirely with The United States Department of War. During World War I, the naming of United States camps and posts was a delicate issue as the nation was still healing after the American Civil War. Brigadier General Joseph Kuhn, Chief of the General Staff's War College, proposed a vague policy that "The names should honor officers who had a connection to the region and who were "not unpopular" in the area."[123]

The use of such names was applauded in the spirit of reconciliation, though it continued to be an ongoing process. In some cases, officials actively sought to name camps after Confederate commanders if Southern divisions were to be housed there." https://www.latimes.com/opinion/story/2021-10-14/civil-war-base-names-confederate-generals.[124]

Ft. Benning in Georgia, for instance, was named after Confederate Gen. Henry L. Benning because the U.S. secretary of War accepted the recommendation of the local chapters of the United Daughters of the Confederacy and the Rotary Club.[125]

As the nation prepared for World War II, Army Regulation 210-10, dated 1 July 1939, established a formal policy on naming installations. General George C. Marshall gave the commanders of the Armed Forces a voice in the selection of naming camps and posts: "the person should be identified with the locality of the post by birth or distinguished service."[126]

This was almost verbatim to Brigadier General Joseph Kuhn's guidelines earlier during World War I, which enabled military installations to be named after Confederate officers.

Fast forward to the death of George Floyd in 2020, which prompted the discussion of redesignating military assets bearing the names of military leaders who served in the Confederacy—men who used their best efforts to maintain and perpetuate the system of slavery that espoused beliefs contrary to the framers of the Constitution that "All men are created Equal." As a result, The Naming Commission was created by the United States Congress in 2021, and a proposal for redesignating was included in the annual National Defense Authorization Act (NDAA) for fiscal year 2021, a defense appropriations bill. Members of the Naming Commission included respected persons from diverse

---

123 https://www.latimes.com/opinion/story/2021-10-14/civil-war-base-names-confederate-generals

124 https://www.latimes.com/opinion/story/2021-10-14/civil-war-base-names-confederate-generals

125 https://www.latimes.com/opinion/story/2021-10-14/civil-war-base-names-confederate-generals

126 https://history.army.mil/faq/naming-of-us-army-posts.htm

ethnicities, gender, and military experience with the goal of reviewing the possibility of changing the names of military bases honoring Confederate Officers.

At the outset, the Naming Commission faced a major obstacle with a veto by former President Donald Trump, who opposed the renaming of the bases. However, the United States House (December 28, 2020) and Senate (January 1, 2021) both voted to override the veto; this was the "first veto override by Congress in the Trump presidency."[127]

The Naming Commission made a report on May 24, 2022, recommending nine new names for Army bases that honored the Confederacy. Defense Secretary Lloyd Austin said in a statement that the recommendations "Reflect the courage, values, sacrifices, and diversity of our military men and women."[128]

Currently Fort Hood in Texas, a major military installation, was redesignated on May 9, 2023, to Fort Cavazos, in honor of General Richard Edward Cavazos, who was the first Hispanic four-star general in the United States Army. Fort Bragg in North Carolina, one of the largest military installations in the world, was redesignated to Fort Liberty on June 2, 2023.

The Pentagon will have until early 2024 to carry out the commission's suggestions along with other recommendations regarding the "750 Department of Defense items identified for review to determine whether their names commemorate the Confederacy."[129]

UNITED STATES SERVICE ACADEMIES

It is imperative that redesignated buildings and monuments at our service academies also reflect people of character who opposed slavery. Our service academies once even struggled with admitting African Americans. After being enrolled, these cadets and midshipmen endured psychological and, in some cases, physical abuse. However, they endured, and many became senior officers.

United States Military Academy West Point has removed Confederate monuments which included a portrait of Robert E. Lee in a Confederate uniform, "A stone bust of his likeness, bronze plaques dedicated to him and other Confederate figures, and a gate, road, and series of academic facilities bearing his name." https://www.cbsnews.com/news/west-point-removes-confederate-symbols-stat-

---

127 https://www.npr.org/2021/01/01/952450018/congress-overturns-trump-veto-on-defense-bill-after-political-detour

128 https://www.politico.com/news/2022/05/24/commission-recommends-nine-new-names-for-army-bases-that-honor-confederates-00034799

129 https://time.com/6180832/military-bases-remove-confederate-names-history/

ues-robert-e-lee/ The United States Naval Academy is taking the same approach with "recommendations to rename two buildings and one street at the U.S. Naval Academy in Annapolis that are named for individuals with Confederate ties." https://chesapeakebaymagazine.com/3-naval-academy-name-changes-recommended-due-to-confederate-ties/

The resignation of building and removing monuments is history correcting itself. "The commissioners do not make these recommendations with any intention of 'erasing history." https://www.military.com/daily-news/2022/08/29/west-point-and-naval-academy-should-scrub-names-of-confederate-officers-panel-tells-congress.html

Martin Luther King, Jr., in a speech given at the National Cathedral, March 31, 1968, reminded us that "the arc of the moral universe is long, but it bends toward justice." Until we have conversations regarding the evils of injustice that permeates all aspects of our society and seek action steps to educate and improve ourselves, we will continue to be disappointed, but not surprised with history often repeating itself.

THE CONFEDERATE FLAG

The Confederate flag has been a longstanding symbol of controversy in the United States. Multiple polls and national surveys consistently support the same, with reported reactions from the display of the flag ranging from racism and southern pride to indifference. Along racial lines, the majority of African Americans perceive the Confederate flag as a symbol of racism, while many whites, especially from southern states, embrace the flag with pride. A historical contextualization of the Confederate flag will lend generously to its true meaning and symbolism.[130]

President Lincoln, in his second inaugural address during the final days of the Civil War, attempted to reunite the nation when he said,

"With malice toward none; with charity for all; with firmness in the right, as God gives us to see the right, let us strive on to finish the work we are in; to bind up the nation's wounds; to care for him who shall have borne the battle, and for his widow, and his orphan—to do all which may achieve and cherish a just, and a lasting peace, among ourselves, and with all nations." March 4, 1865

Despite the olive branch and sincere optimism of the president after the

---

130 https://en.wikipedia.org/wiki/Modern_display_of_the_Confederate_battle_flag

fall of Richmond, VA, and the surrender at Appomattox, VA, many southerners embraced the "Lost Cost" ideology: The Union violated their states' rights guaranteed in the United States Constitution, and the war was not about slavery. During this post-Civil War era, the battle flag of General Robert E. Lee's Army of Northern Virginia became a symbol of the Confederacy. The Confederate States of America had three different national flags from 1861 to 1865, and multiple other flags were used by individual states, armies, and naval groups. Lee's battle flag rose to prominence and was recognized by its red background and blue X with 13 white stars. The stars represented the 11 Confederate states and Missouri and Kentucky, though they never officially seceded.

Some states incorporated the battle flag as a part of their state flag. Ironically, "In 1895, Alabama adopted a state flag that used the St. Andrew's Cross from the CBF at the same time that it was passing segregation laws. Florida adopted a similar type of flag in 1900. In 1894, Mississippi adopted a flag that included the CBF."[131]

The battle flag became an iconic symbol for such organizations as United Confederate Veterans, Sons of Confederate Veterans, and United Daughters of the Confederacy. It was also used extensively by the Ku Klux Klan, white supremacists, and segregationists in defense of Jim Crow. It emerged as a political symbol in 1948, when a new political party of Southerners opposed Harry S. Truman and the Democratic Party's position on civil rights and Truman's goal of integrating the United States military. They became known as "Dixiecrats" and adopted the Confederate battle flag as their party's emblem and the platform for states' rights. The flag was clearly associated with opposition to civil rights and the government's intrusion into the lives of individuals.

While pastoring in Mississippi, I participated in public dialogue regarding the battle flag. In 2001, a flag referendum was on the ballot. Before the actual date of the vote, both sides discussed the flag in public forums. I invited the late Mississippi Governor, William Winter, who led the commission that designed a new flag, to speak at my church in Jackson, Mississippi. He shared that his deceased grandfather had been a Confederate soldier but that it was time to change the flag. However, the referendum was defeated.

Winter shared that while he was disappointed in the voting results, he was encouraged by how many voters had supported what he called "a symbol of

---

131 https://roanoke.com/opinion/reed-the-confederate-battle-flag-is-a-symbol-of-resistance/article_0458e9e5-1622-53e6-8566-b3888b960cea.html

unity," increasing the possibility of a new state flag. Nineteen years later, Mississippi lawmakers voted, in June 2020, to retire the state's Confederate flag and adopt a new design, which will be inclusive of all people. Governor Tate Reeves of Mississippi said of the vote, "A flag is a symbol of our past, our present, and our future. For those reasons, we need a new symbol."[132]

The battle flag celebrates a cause that, had it succeeded, would have continued slavery for generations in the 11 Confederate States of America for approximately 4 million people. America is still healing from the past wounds of slavery, and hoisting the battle flag is counterproductive to the future. Sadly, the battle flag was carried through the halls of the Capitol during the insurrection. Such a symbol should be consigned to a museum like Confederate statues that honor those who embraced and fought to preserve slavery. My wife is a descendant of a Confederate officer, and so it is a part of her family heritage. But, to her, and understandably so, the Confederate flag represents an egregious history of racism and grossly disparate treatment of fellow human beings who were at the center of a civil war for the perpetuation of their enslavement. A flag should unite, not divide people.

CONFEDERATE STATUES

In America, a statue in a public space honors and celebrates the values and deeds of the person. Confederate statues honor persons that endorsed slavery and fought to preserve this societal ill. "The vast majority of them were built between the 1890s and 1950s, which matches up exactly with the era of Jim Crow segregation."[133]

In a combined effort to preserve and perpetuate their beliefs, White supremacists and segregationists solicited organizations to raise funds for erecting these statutes, which have increased exponentially over the years. According to the Southern Poverty Law Center 2016 report, there were about 1,503 symbols of the Confederacy in public spaces and 109 public schools named after prominent Confederates, many of which have large African-American student populations. There were more than 700 Confederate monuments and statues on public property throughout the country, the vast majority in the South. As of September 2022 "In three reports, the Naming Commission has identified more than 800 items honoring the Confederacy on military property. ...they are located in 20 states and Washington, D.C.—as well as Germany and Japan..."[134] Also, there

132 https://www.washingtonpost.com/national/mississippi-flag-confederacy-removed/2020/06/30

133 https://www.history.com/news/how-the-u-s-got-so-many-confederate-monuments

134 https://www.splcenter.org/news/2022/09/20/federal-report-removal-confederacy-military-bases

are nine Confederate holidays or observances in six Southern states.

These statutes glorify those who fought for the preservation of the southern lifestyle and culture that included slavery. The Constitution of the Confederate States opened the door to their beliefs:

Article I, Section 9, Clause 4 prohibited the Confederate government from restricting slavery in any way: "No bill of attainder, ex post facto law, or law denying or impairing the right of property in negro slaves shall be passed."

Article IV, Section 2, prohibited states from interfering with slavery: "The citizens of each State shall be entitled to all the privileges and immunities of citizens in the several States; and shall have the right of transit and sojourn in any State of this Confederacy, with their slaves and other property; and the right of property in said slaves shall not be thereby impaired."

Article IV, Section 3, Clause 3 protected the future of slavery in future territories conquered or acquired by the Confederacy "The Confederate States may acquire new territory; and Congress shall have the power to legislate and provide governments for the inhabitants of all territories belonging to the Confederate States, lying without the limits of the several States; and may permit them, at such times, and in such manner as it may by law provide, to form states to be admitted into the Confederacy. In all such territory, the institution of negro slavery, as it now exists in the Confederate States, shall be recognized and protected by Congress and by the Territorial government; and the inhabitants of the several Confederate States and Territories shall have the right to take to such Territory any slaves lawfully held by them in any of the States or Territories of the Confederate States."

The words of men who served in leadership roles in the Confederacy represented an indictment against the values of the founding fathers that are so profoundly amplified in the Declaration of Independence: "We hold these truths to be self-evident, that all men are created equal, that they are endowed by their Creator with certain unalienable Rights, that among these are Life, Liberty and the pursuit of Happiness."

Referencing slaves, United States Senator Jefferson Davis, later President of the Confederacy, said, "We recognize the fact of the inferiority stamped upon that race of men by the Creator, and from the cradle to the grave, our Government, as a civil institution, marks that inferiority." United States Senate Chamber, February 29, 1860. Alexander Stephens, vice president of the Confederacy, said: "[Our new government's] foundations are laid, its cornerstone rests, upon the great truth that the negro is not equal to the white man."[135]

Confederate General Robert E. Lee, in a letter to his wife, wrote, "The blacks are immeasurably better off here than in Africa, morally, socially & physically," and their "painful discipline," as slaves will "prepare & lead them to better things."[136]

The progress of the removal of these statutes continues, as the United States House of Representatives voted on June 29, 2021, to remove all Confederate statues from public display in the United States Capitol. House of Representatives bill House Resolution 3005 proposes the following: "To direct the Joint Committee on the Library to replace the bust of Roger Brooke Taney in the Old Supreme Court Chamber of the United States Capitol with a bust of Thurgood Marshall to be obtained by the Joint Committee on the Library and to remove certain statues from areas of the United States Capitol which are accessible to the public, to remove all statues of individuals who voluntarily served the Confederate States of America from display in the United States Capitol, and for other purposes."

Prior to this action, the statue of General Robert E. Lee was removed from the United States Capitol's Statuary Hall collection on December 21, 2020, and replaced by a statue honoring civil rights activist Barbara Johns of Virginia.

Contrary to the claim of many, the removal of Confederate statues is not an attempt to erase history but rather to allow the monuments to more accurately reflect the history linked to them. Confederate monuments might serve a better purpose in museums where they can be studied in the context of slavery, the Confederacy, the Civil War, and the Jim Crow Era.

STONES OF REMEMBRANCE: LEARNING FROM HISTORY

Despite multiple barriers and disparities, African American history is a story of triumph over obstacles, which were impossible without the hand of God stirring the pot of human history. The book of Joshua (chapters 3-5) records the inspiring story of the Israelites crossing the flood-staged Jordan river through God's miraculous power and supports the above belief. The Jordan river was the only physical barrier between them and the promised land. The culmination of this journey offered relief from forty years of desert wandering and countless funerals due to disobedience, not to mention the traumatic experience of slavery

135 https://www.npr.org/2017/08/20/544266880/confederate-statues-were-built-to-further-a-white-supremacist-future
136 https://encyclopediavirginia.org/entries/lee-robert-e-and-slavery/

while in Egypt. When the feet of the priests who carried the "Ark of the Covenant" touched the water's edge, the river miraculously parted, and the priests stood firmly in the middle of the Jordan until all the people had safely crossed over the river's dry pathway.

Before the crossing of the Jordan, God instructed Joshua, "Take for yourselves twelve men from the people, one man from every tribe, and command them, saying, 'Take for yourselves twelve stones from here, out of the midst of the Jordan, from the place where the priests' feet stood firm." (Joshua 4:2-3). The purpose was to build a monument with stones commemorating God's awesome power in parting the Jordan so that when future generations asked, "What do these stones mean to you?" Joshua 4:6, the Hebrews would be able to share the nation's history. That history includes the miraculous dividing of the Red Sea, being guided through the desert by a cloud by day and a pillar of fire at night, being fed by manna from heaven, and, as they prepared to enter the Promised Land, the supernatural parting of the Jordan—all precious stones of remembrance.

Throughout African American history, God has used men and women to collect stones of remembrance that continue to serve as a beacon of light that leads to a brighter tomorrow. The 21st century has produced some colossal stones of remembrance with the election of Barack Obama, the 44th President of the United States; Kamala Harris, the 49th Vice President of the United States; and Pastor Raphael Warnock, Georgia's first African American United States Senator.

Despite these remarkable stones of remembrance, the nation is still grappling with its past issues of slavery and inequities. However, African American history has phenomenal potential to continue producing stones of remembrance as it educates and heightens awareness. Without African American history, the story of American history is incomplete. As the ancient stones from the Jordan were a witness of God's providential care and protection, African American history produces stones of remembrance that serve as memoirs of God's goodness, compassion, grace, and love toward African Americans and all people with whom He desires to live eternally.

STONES OF REMEMBRANCE: FEDERAL HOLIDAYS

On June 16, 2021, the United States Congress voted to make Juneteenth the first new federal holiday since Martin Luther King Jr. Day in 1983, which has become known as "a day on rather than a day off." All Americans are encouraged to participate in some form of volunteer community service on the King holiday. Another federal holiday of historical significance, Juneteenth (short for June Nineteenth), was signed into law by President Joseph Biden on June 17, 2021. Juneteenth traces its roots back to the American Civil War, when, on June 19, 1865, Major General Gordon Granger and 2,000 federal troops arrived in Galveston, Texas, to officially free slaves still held in bondage in the last Southern state in open rebellion. The slaves listened as General Order No. 3 was read: "The people of Texas are informed that, in accordance with a proclamation from the Executive of the United States, all slaves are free." Afterward they offered prayers of gratitude to the God of Heaven, sang celebratory songs, and danced for joy, as the Israelites did after crossing the Red Sea following their deliverance from Egypt.

This celebration, however, should have occurred two years earlier since the Emancipation Proclamation had been issued by President Abraham Lincoln on January 1, 1863. It stated that enslaved people in Confederate states in rebellion against the Union "shall be then, thenceforward, and forever free." The Governor of Texas and citizens refused to recognize the sovereignty of the federal government and continued to enslave African Americans, withholding the news of General Robert E. Lee surrendering to General Ulysses S. Grant at Appomattox Court House on April 9, 1865.

During the Civil War, slavery thrived in Texas, as many slave owners from Arkansas, Louisiana, and Mississippi, brought their slaves to Texas to wait out the war. Some of these slave owners forced their former slaves off their plantations with only the clothes they were wearing. Others promised them fair wages, improved working and living conditions, and sharecropping (another form of slavery), but these promises were often broken. Fortunately, those able to leave went for better economic opportunities, while others went in search of family members separated through slavery. On the other hand, there were many who freely left the plantations without restraint because of the compliance of their slave owners.

The Juneteenth holiday was originally celebrated in Texas, but with the migration of former slaves, the celebration traveled with them to their various locations. Juneteenth's celebration has included the reading of the Emancipation Proclamation, sermons, singing of spirituals and Miss Juneteenth contests. These traditions continue today with a few additions, such as picnics, rodeos, cookouts, and family reunions. Scrumptious meals, which include red foods and drinks such as red beans and rice, red velvet cake, red strawberry soda, and watermelon, traditionally comprise many Juneteenth celebration menus. Red symbolizes generations of suffering and resiliency by slaves.

Juneteenth was once referred to as Emancipation Day, Freedom Day, and Jubilee Day, but most importantly, it commemorates the end of slavery in the United States. The holiday encourages reflections on the past and is a day of celebration for all Americans who believe in liberty. It further aligns with Moses' admonition to the Israelites, "Remember the days of old, consider the years of many generations. Ask your father, and he will show you" (Deuteronomy 32:7).

THE STAR OF HOPE: NORTH STAR

The North Star serves as a fixed compass in the night sky, guiding the pathway to the dawning of a new day. The North Star, or Polaris, is located directly above the North Pole. It can be identified at night in the Northern Hemisphere. If you can see the North Star, it is obvious which way is north. The North Star is the brightest star in the constellation Ursa Minor, also known as the Little Dipper, shaped like a "drinking gourd," similar to the one that was used by slaves to dip water. At creation, God created the vast constellations to reflect His majesty and glory. In His omniscience, He knew that slaves would rely on the North star to lead them to freedom.

Harriet Tubman, one of the best-known conductors of the Underground Railroad, a network of safe houses for slaves, while attempting to escape into the free states and Canada, used the North Star as a compass on the journey to freedom. It is estimated that "between 1810 and 1850, the Underground Railroad helped to guide one hundred thousand enslaved people to freedom."[137]

The bright rays of the North Star shone upon them from heaven while they attempted to steer clear of being captured, as they were subject to the Fugitive Slave Act of 1850. However, several mainstream denominations, especially the Religious Society of Friends (Quakers), played a pivotal role in the success of the Underground Railroad.

The North Star continually symbolized hope. Some years later, in 1906, Charles Albert Tindley (1850-1933), a Methodist minister, wrote lyrics in the hymn, "Beams of Heaven," (formerly called "Someday") seemingly to encourage hope for African Americans during some of the most arduous times of their journeys and to acknowledge the oppression they faced as they migrated to northern cities.

---

137 https://education.nationalgeographic.org/resource/underground-railroad

The lyrics also alluded to the Israelites' exodus from Egypt and the "Star of Hope" that appeared at the birth of Christ. The lyrics encouraged a focus on the beams of heaven, as did the slaves on the North Star, in anticipation of both the earthly and heavenly promised land.

Beams of heaven as I go,
through the wilderness below,
guide my feet in peaceful ways,
turn my midnights into days.

When in the darkness, I would grope,
faith always sees a star of hope,
and soon, from all life's grief and danger
I shall be free someday.

Refrain:
I do not know how long 'twill be,
nor what the future holds for me,
but this I know: if Jesus leads me,
I shall get home someday.[138]

The biblical record confirms that God is the Creator of the vast constellations and has used them to unveil His liberating and redemptive purposes:

"Then God made two great lights: the greater light to rule the day, and the lesser light to rule the night. He made the stars also." (Genesis 1:16).

"And the LORD went before them by day in a pillar of cloud to lead the way, and by night in a pillar of fire to give them light, so as to go by day and night." (Exodus 13:21).

"When I consider Your heavens, the work of Your fingers, The moon and the stars, which You have ordained." (Psalm 8:3).

"A Star shall come out of Jacob; A Scepter shall rise out of Israel." (Numbers 24:17).

"Lift up your eyes on high, And see who has created these things, Who brings out their host by number; He calls them all by name, By the greatness of

---

138 https://www.umcdiscipleship.org/resources/history-of-hymns-beams-of-heaven-as-i-go

His might And the strength of His power; Not one is missing." (Isaiah 40:26).

"Where is He who has been born King of the Jews? For we have seen His star in the East and have come to worship Him." (Matthew 2:2).

The angelic host appeared as a bright star to the shepherds and announced the birth of Jesus "Glory to God in the highest, And on earth peace, goodwill toward men!" (Luke 2:4).

The history of African Americans is filled with numerous North Stars who have contributed to the betterment of society for all people. Fortunately, this growing list continues into the 21st century:

- Lloyd James Austin III- the 28th United States Secretary of Defense and the first African American to serve in the position, and a retired United States Army four-star general.

- Ketanji Brown Jackson- the first African American female associate justice of the Supreme Court of the United States.

- Barry C. Black- the 62nd chaplain of the United States Senate, first African-American to serve in this post; retired United States Navy rear admiral (upper half); first African-American United States Navy Chief of Chaplains.

- Kizzmekia Corbett- an African American immunologist at the Harvard Radcliffe Institute who previously served at the National Institutes of Health's Vaccine Research Center (VRC) as the scientific lead on the VRC's Covid-19 team that was responsible for developing the Moderna COVID-19 vaccine.

- United States House Representative, Hakeem Jeffries (D)- New York's 8th Congressional District, is the first African American to head a major political party in the 118th United States Congress, serving as House Minority Leader.

- Sonceria "Ann" Bishop Berry- the 34th Secretary of the United States Senate and the first African American to hold the position in the 117th United States Congress.

The achievements of these men and women continue to inspire us; however, the ultimate reward of eternal life promised to the faithful believers in God will be given—at the second coming of Christ. We will also receive a crown with stars from Jesus Christ, the One who made the North Star and is our eternal Star of Hope.

"And they that be wise shall shine as the brightness of the firmament; and they that turn many to righteousness as the stars forever and ever." (Daniel 12:3).

AN EPIC STORY OF AFRICAN AMERICAN MIGRATION

From 1910-1970s, African Americans migrated from the south to escape segregation and fair better economically. Between 1915 and 1916, cotton production decreased in the south due to "crop damage from the boll weevil"[139]

It is estimated over the previous decades that "approximately six million Black people moved from the American South to Northern, Midwestern, and Western states."[140]

The north was viewed as "a land flowing with milk and honey." (Exodus 3:8). This perception existed primarily because, in the northern cities, employment was more readily available. Though the work was industrial and often backbreaking with long hours, the wages superseded three times what southerners had earned as sharecroppers.

During this period, many African Americans migrated from Alabama, Mississippi and Tennessee to northern cities such as New York City, Chicago, Cleveland, and Detroit. This first wave of migrates was filled with determination and succeeded despite the cold temperatures, subtle and sometimes overt discrimination, overcrowded landscape, and rising crime. Unfortunately, some migrants also experienced permanent family separation, as men would occasionally migrate ahead of the family to establish new homes with promises to return for the entire family but failed to do so.

Employment opportunities for African Americans arose in unique ways. With the outbreak of World War I around 1914, there was a shortage of factory workers, and African Americans were hired and worked in southern manufacturing facilities and assembly plants. In the north, they became entrepreneurs and property owners. They gave birth to the Harlem Renaissance in New York City, which became known as the African American cultural mecca in the early 20th Century. Across many other cities, a social and artistic explosion ensued for African Americans.

---

139 https://www.britannica.com/event/Great-Migration

140 https://www.archives.gov/research/african-americans/migrations/great-migration

However, African American migration decreased "considerably in the 1930s, when the country sank into the Great Depression."[141]

Depression lasted from approximately 1929 to 1939 and affected everyone living in the United States at that time. However, "…few suffered more than African Americans. Said to be "last hired, first fired," African Americans were the first to see hours and jobs cut, and they experienced the highest unemployment rate during the 1930s. Since they were already relegated to lower-paying professions, African Americans had less of a financial cushion to fall back on when the economy collapsed."[142]

Sadly, the impact of The Great Depression would affect African Americans for many decades thereafter. They would need to fight constantly for basic civil liberties, i.e., the right to vote, desegregation, etc., eventually spurring the notable Civil Rights Movement of the 1950s and1960s.

The second wave of migration followed the attack on Pearl Harbor on December 7, 1941, when the nation entered World War II. Once again, there was an urgent need for factory workers in the war effort. During this period, African Americans migrated westward from Texas and Louisiana to Oakland, Los Angeles, and San Francisco, and the north Pacific to Portland and Seattle. However, it should be noted that African Americans had traveled westward earlier during the California gold rush of 1849. Additionally, "African Americans were among the pioneers who crossed the trail to Oregon, some coming willingly as free men and women, but others forced to travel as the property of slaveholders."[143]

More westward and mid-westward migrations occurred during the 1870s when African Americans "settled in Kansas, but many settled in what would become Oklahoma, Colorado, Ohio, Nebraska, North Dakota, South Dakota, New Mexico, Arizona, and Montana."[144]

While these migrations were farther from the south, they were profitable, allowing for increased earnings, warmer climates, more affluent lifestyles, and exposure to different industries such as shipbuilding. Despite these advantages, they still encountered ongoing discrimination among those who had migrated north earlier.

---

141 https://www.history.com/topics/black-history/great-migration

142 https://www.history.com/news/last-hired-first-fired-how-the-great-depression-affected-african-americans

143 https://www.nps.gov/articles/000/african-americans-on-the-oregon-trail.htm

144 https://www.archives.gov/research/african-americans/migrations/exodusters

During the 50s and 60s, African Americans continued to migrate to the Rust Belt, being hired in the steel industry and automotive manufacturing plants. However, over time with the decline of production due to less expensive foreign competition, cities such as Buffalo, Cleveland, Detroit, Gary, and Pittsburgh experienced higher-than-normal unemployment rates.

Starting with the deindustrialization and the Rust Belt crisis, African Americans in the 70s began to experience "the reversal of the Great Migration."[145]

Contributing factors included the accessibility of Historically Black Colleges and Universities in the south, allowing the children and grandchildren of earlier migrants to be educated in a post-civil rights era. The opportunities denied to their forebears were opened to them. Additional opportunities came during the late 70s and onward, where African Americans were elected in the south as mayors of major cities, state legislators, judges, and CEOs of companies. Further, several African American religious denominations were headquartered in the south, often drawing constituents to reside in close proximity.

The lower cost of living compared to other areas, the growing African American middle-class and southern hospitality also contributed to the return of many African Americans to the south. This positive trend of African Americans reclaiming their roots in the south is a testimony of God's power to change the hearts and lives of people and the nation.

Those who first migrated to the north soon discovered that the northern cities did not portray their Beulah land as proclaimed by the prophet Isaiah: "You shall no longer be termed Forsaken, Nor shall your land any more be termed Desolate; But you shall be called Hephzibah, and your land Beulah; For the Lord delights in you, And your land shall be married. For as a young man marries a virgin, So shall your sons marry you; And as the bridegroom rejoices over the bride, So shall your God rejoice over you." (Isaiah 62:4-5). Isaiah is speaking here of the time when Israel will return from the Babylonian exile and once again return to the Lord. In Hebrew, Beulah means "married," and is applied to the land that the people of Israel will marry. People of faith should look forward anxiously to the heavenly Beulah land, from which there will be no departure, but victory, rest, safety, and eternal fellowship with God! Fannie Crosby, the prolific hymnologist and abolitionist, said it best in the lyrics of the song, "I have Entered Beulah Land:"[146]

---

145 https://www.brookings.edu/research/a-new-great-migration-is-bringing-black-americans-back-to-the-south
146 https://hymnary.org/text/o_my_cup_is_overflowing

Oh, my cup is overflowing with the goodness of the Lord;
I am trusting in His mercy and rejoicing in His Word.

I have climbed the rugged mountain; on its summit now I stand;
Hallelujah! Hallelujah! I have entered Beulah Land.

From the sighing and the longing that so oft my heart oppressed;
With my Savior and Redeemer now in perfect peace I rest.

There' a palace over the river, and its Jasper walls I see.
And among its many mansions, there is one prepared for me.

I have climbed the rugged mountain, but my Savior led the way.
Unto Him shall be the glory, when I reach eternal day.

REFLECTING MORE ON THE TOPIC:

What were your most meaningful takeaways from this chapter?

____

____

____

____

What will you do differently because of your increased awareness?

____

____

____

____

What resources or support do you need to ensure the successful achievement of your goals?

____

____

____

____

CHAPTER 7

EMBRACING UNITY IN DIVERSITY

In the United States, people of varied backgrounds, i.e., religious, racial, ethnic, cultural, socioeconomic, etc., live, work, worship, and socialize together, demonstrating a semblance of unity in diversity or oneness. However, overt racism continues to taint the relationship between dissimilar persons who desire to celebrate their differences. Enforced racism or racial discrimination can adversely impact large segments of persons of color in multiple areas, i.e., housing, education, socioeconomic disadvantage, etc.

RACISM

"Racism leads to religious wars, denigration of women and children, the horror of ethnic cleansing, slavery, criminal actions against indigenous peoples, clan and civil wars, and gross violations of civil and human rights."[147]

In an extreme case of racism, my uncle was almost lynched as a teenager as he was walking home from visiting friends. Two male perpetrators had a noose around my uncle's neck when suddenly, their boss called them on a walkie-talkie and said, "Whatever you are doing, stop right now and head back to the shop because we need to close early today." My uncle had committed no crime or any infraction. He was guilty of being an African American, God-fearing man. The ugliness of racism was clearly at work but countered by God's protective care that kept my uncle from an earlier death.

Equally bleak is another story shared by my parents of when my mother gave birth to my younger brother, Grayland. On the day my mother and brother were discharged from the hospital, a massive protest against the scheduled integration of a predominately white high school nearby blocked the city streets. The protesters were in such large numbers that police officers would not allow people to go through the roadblock after 10 a.m. each day unless they had an official permit, which my father did not have. However, my grandfather, a mortician, proposed using one of his hearses to get through the barricade. Fortunately,

147 https://baptist-atlantic.ca/wp-content/uploads/2012/02/sin_of_racism.pdf

with no questions asked, he was allowed to bypass the policemen and transport my mother and brother safely home, though in the front seat of a hearst.

Unfortunately, racism, racial discrimination, and prejudice are as ancient as the Bible. Acts Chapter 10 sheds light on the struggle to overcome prejudiced feelings toward others in the body of Christ. The story begins with a devout God-fearing Roman Army officer, Cornelius, who prayerfully worships the true God of heaven to the best of his abilities. While he was praying for more profound spiritual insight, an angel said, "Your prayers and your alms have come up for a memorial before God." (Acts 10:4). God prompts Cornelius in a vision to send some men to Joppa to invite Peter to his home in Caesarea, although for Peter, it would be earth-shaking to lodge and eat in a Gentile's home. Cornelius' men immediately prepared to travel to Joppa and arrived the next day.

Meanwhile, Peter was a guest at Simon's house, and during the afternoon, Peter went on the flat roof to find some quiet time to pray while awaiting the meal to be prepared. Suddenly, he had a vision of a vast sheet that descended from heaven. It contained all kinds of four-footed animals, as well as reptiles and birds. Then a voice told him, "Get up, Peter. Kill and eat. But Peter said, Not so, Lord! For I have never eaten anything common or unclean. And a voice spoke to him again the second time, "What God has cleansed you must not call common." This experience happened three times before the object went up into heaven again. (Acts 10:12-16).

Peter's vision was clearly not about eating unclean food because the Bible, in Leviticus 11 and Deuteronomy 14, distinguishes between clean and unclean animals Rather, this passage offers an illustration of Peter's prejudices toward persons who were dissimilar to himself. God was speaking to him about his apprehension of embracing Gentiles on both spiritual and social levels.

Peter was present at Pentecost, where he preached an incredible sermon resulting in three thousand people deciding to follow Jesus Christ. Deep within, he harbored feelings of prejudice and discrimination that would not only hinder the spread of the gospel but adversely affect his relationship with the compassionate Jesus on whom his sermons centered.

Peter knew what was right but did not want to offend the religious leaders. While he was trying to figure out his vision, three men sent by Cornelius arrived where he was staying and shared the reason for their visit. Peter agreed to go back with them to Caesarea and explain the Gospel of Jesus Christ to Cornelius' household. The Holy Spirit descended upon them, and they were all baptized.

Fortunately, Peter was willing to make the gospel practical in his life.

No one is immune to prejudice. The real danger is when it results in behaviors that cause others to feel inferior, discriminated against, and undervalued. Both a theorethical and practical understanding of racism dynamics can potentially contribute to improved racial relations. However, at the end of the day it is God's power alone that can transform a prejudiced heart and mind into one that loves and accepts all people. If His service is to be moved forward effectively, this transformative work must be imperative.

MICROAGGRESSION

The Americal Psychological Association describes microagression as "brief and commonplace verbal, behavioral, or situational indignities that communicate hostile, derogatory, or negative slights or insults, especially toward members of minority or oppressed groups." https://dictionary.apa.org/microaggression

Microaggression was "coined in 1970 by Harvard University psychiatrist Chester Pierce." https://blogs.scientificamerican.com/observations/the-science-of-microaggressions-its-complicated/ Examples of microaggression include phrases such as: "Anyone can succeed if they/you work hard enough," "You are so articulate," "Is that your real hair?" Microaggression can also be nonverbal: when person (s) prefers to take the next elevator, stand on public transportation rather than taking a seat beside a person of color, and following persons of color around in a store.

However, there are ways to respond to microaggression:
- Seek to understand and then to be understood. Clarification will give the microaggression initiator(s) an opportunity to explain their comments or behavior.

- Provide honest and clear feedback in a non-antagonistic way.

- Express your feelings at the appropriate time and do not allow them to build up and explode.

- Challenge stereotypical statements with probing questions such as, "why are you saying I am so articulate?".

- Debrief by sharing your experience with another person(s).

Not confronting the issue will not solve the issue and can lead to emotional numbness or apathetic dispositions about an issue that requires ongoing vigilance.

CRITICAL RACE THEORY

Critical Race Theory (CRT) has developed into a controversial flashcard in the nation, causing school boards, state legislatures, and even church members to cringe. Critical Race Theory has been erroneously identified as being divisive. The term CRT was coined by Kimberlé Crenshaw, a professor at the UCLA School of Law and Columbia Law School. She is also credited with deriving the related concept of intersectionality, described by the Oxford Dictionary as "the interconnected nature of social categorizations such as race, class, and gender, regarded as creating overlapping and interdependent systems of discrimination or disadvantage."

CRT is an idea that was conceived in the aftermath of the American Civil Rights movement. Even with laws in place against segregation, there was still apparent structural and systemic racism creating differential outcomes for African Americans. Derrick Bell, a lawyer, professor, and civil rights activist in the 1970s, along with other legal scholars, "Alan Freemen and Richard Delgado, began developing alternative legal theories and frameworks for combating racial inequality."[148]

Critical Race Theory was the "lens through which these legal scholars could analyze policies and the law."[149]

Some critics have attempted to associate CRT with Marxism, as both are social sciences that critique society. However, there are major differences "Marxism focuses on material wealth and is far more radical in its calls for revolution."[150]

As a nation, we cannot rewrite history, for it is forever sketched in the archives of time and will always speak the truth of which it is comprised. Some, however, would like to alter many of the dark historical truths that have brought disgrace to this nation. For example, the Texas Education Agency, which is responsible for setting curricula state-wide, discussed substituting the word slavery for "involuntary relocation," a description that greatly dilutes the horrific truth about this unthinkable thralldom.[151]

There are many divergent views regarding CRT that require an open mind for an accurate understanding. Simply put, CRT is an attempt to understand

148 https://www.mtsu.edu/first-amendment/article/1254/critical-race-theory

149 https://www.vox.com/2020/9/24/21451220/critical-race-theory-diversity-training-trump

150 https://www.denisonforum.org/resources/is-critical-race-theory-marxist/

151 https://www.cbsnews.com/news/texas-education-officials-proposed-changing-slavery-to-involuntary-relocation-for-second-grade-standards/

the past while facing the future with optimism. The same theme was heard in the first inaugural address of President Barack Obama. "For we know that our patchwork heritage is a strength, not a weakness. We are a nation of Christians and Muslims, Jews and Hindus, and non-believers. We are shaped by every language and culture, drawn from every end of this Earth, and because we have tasted the bitter swill of civil war and segregation and emerged from that dark chapter stronger and more united, we cannot help but believe that the old hatreds shall someday pass; that the lines of tribe shall soon dissolve; that as the world grows smaller, our common humanity shall reveal itself; and that America must play its role in ushering in a new era of peace." January 21, 2009.

RACISM ROOTED IN SIN

Sin is the ultimate cause of racism in our world and should be a concern for everyone, especially people of faith. Where did sin originate? There are many attempts to explain sin. In Greek Mythology, Pandora opens a container, and out comes the forces of evil, death, and sickness. After she was unsuccessful in putting the evil, believed to be the result of sin, back into the container, the myth ascertains these evils went into the world.

The Bible gives an accurate account of sin's origin. This cosmic struggle between good and evil is more action-packed than Star Wars. John the Revelator opened the curtains to a drama that begins with these words: "Then war broke out in heaven. Michael and his angels fought against the dragon, and the dragon and his angels fought back. But he was not strong enough, and they lost their place in heaven." (Revelation 12:7-8). Satan (the dragon) was once an angel in heaven who, over time and without cause, became jealous of Jesus. Even though God created a perfect universe based on divine love and obedience principles, Satan became disloyal and jealous of God's son, resulting in a war that disrupted heaven.

His unjust attacks against the character of God led to open rebellion and permanent expulsion from heaven, along with sympathetic angels (one-third of the heavenly host) who succumbed to his deceptions. The Bible says of Satan, "Your heart became proud on account of your beauty, and you corrupted your wisdom because of your splendor." (Ezekiel 28:17). Unfortunately, Satan did not give up there but continued to spread rebellion on earth. Disguised as a speaking serpent, using the same arguments that had led to his downfall in heaven, he effectively undermined Adam and Eve's trust in God: "He said to the woman, 'Did God really say, you must not eat from any tree in the garden?'" (Genesis 3:5). The impact of eating the forbidden fruit plunged the entire human race into a crisis and brokenness, resulting in all kinds of evils, including racism, which seems to prominently manifest itself in both likely and unlikely places, i.e., places of worship. It immediately created the need for a complete restoration, which fortunately resulted in the death and resurrection of Christ.

AN UNLIKELY PLACE FOR RACISM

The church should be the one place above all others where classism, colorism, prejudice, and privilege do not exist. But it does, resulting in the establishment of several African American denominations such as The African Methodist Episcopal Church (1816), The Christian Methodist Episcopal Church (1870), The Cumberland Presbyterian Church in America (1874), The National Baptist Convention, USA, Inc. (1880). The Church of God in Christ (1897). The Seventh-day Adventist Church established separate African American regional conferences but remained a part of their denomination. This action was authorized by the denomination's "General Conference Spring Council in 1944."[152]

Clergy and members must be intentional in creating an atmosphere that epitomizes the words of Jesus in Matthew 25:45: "I say to you, in as much as you did not do it to one of the least of these, you did not do it to Me." Before the Civil War, some clergy supported segregation right from the pulpit, even though it is utterly contrary to the Bible. Other "defenders of slavery argued that the institution was divine and that it brought Christianity to the heathen from across the ocean."[153]

Here are a few of their misinterpreted scriptures in favor of slavery:
Canaan, Ham's son, was made a slave to his brothers (Genesis 9:24–27).

Abraham, the "father of faith," and all the patriarchs, held slaves without God's disapproval (Genesis 21:9–10).

The Ten Commandments mention slavery twice, showing God's implicit acceptance of it (Exodus 20:10, 17).

Slavery was widespread throughout the Roman world, and yet Jesus never spoke against it.

The apostle Paul specifically commanded slaves to obey their masters. (Ephesians 6:5–8).

It was a tradition on Sundays for plantation owners to allow slaves to as-

152 https://adventistregionalministries.org/history/

153 https://www.ushistory.org/us/27f.asp

semble for worship: "Oftentimes, slave owners manipulated the word of God to protect the institution of enslavement."[154]

The slave preacher had to strike the right balance between Jesus as their Savior and the requirement to obey the slave master. The most common passages used to validate the latter position was:

"Bondservants, obey in all things your masters according to the flesh, not with eye service, as men-pleasers, but in sincerity of heart, fearing God." (Colossians 3:22).

"Bondservants, be obedient to those who are your masters according to the flesh, with fear and trembling, in sincerity of heart, as to Christ; not with eyeservice, as men-pleasers, but as bondservants of Christ, doing the will of God from the heart, with goodwill doing service, as to the Lord, and not to men, knowing that whatever good anyone does, he will receive the same from the Lord, whether he is a slave or free." (Ephesians 6:5-8).

A SHARED DNA

Through the centuries, evolutionists have challenged the biblical worldview, that God created the earth in seven literal days, according to Genesis 2:1-2, as well as the creation of man in God's image according to Genesis 1:26: "Then God said, "Let Us make man in Our image, according to Our likeness." Evolutionists are proponents of the theory that the earth and humans evolved over millions of years. Some anthropologists also support the belief that man is a Homo sapiens: "Humans are one of more than 200 species belonging to the order of primates."[155]

The origin of evolution traces its roots to a Scottish physician, James Hutton, who wrote a three-volume work in 1795 entitled, *Theory of the Earth*. Later, in 1859, Charles Darwin added his support to the belief of evolution in his book, *On the Origin of Species by Means of Natural Selection, or the Preservation of Favoured Races in the Struggle for Life*. However, the Genesis account of creation clarifies that the first humans created on earth were Adam and his wife, Eve. They were instructed by God to "Be fruitful and multiply" (Genesis 1:28). From Adam and Eve's Deoxyribonucleic Acid (DNA), the human race has a common ancestry. DNA in our cells serves as a blueprint for building and maintaining our anatomy and physiology from conception to death.

Noah and his three sons, Shem, Ham, and Japheth (Genesis 7:13), were

154 https://www.embracerace.org/resources/is-god-racist-or-is-it-my-church

155 https://humanorigins.si.edu/evidence/human-fossils/species/homo-sapiens

descendants of Adam and Eve. After surviving the flood with their wives, "God blessed Noah and his sons, and said to them: "Be fruitful and multiply, and fill the earth." (Genesis 9:1). They had one language and one culture, and the earth repopulated from their genes. The list of the descendants of Noah's sons is in the table of nations in Genesis 10. In Genesis 11, after the flood, men built a tower to protect themselves from a future flood, which displeased God because He had made a covenant with man to never destroy the earth again by a flood, with the rainbow as the visible sign of His promise. (Genesis 9:16). God confused the builders' language to prevent the tower's completion, making it difficult for them to communicate concerning the tower's construction details. "The Lord scattered them abroad from there over the face of all the earth, and they ceased building the city. Therefore, its name is called Babel, because there the Lord confused the language of all the earth; and from there the Lord scattered them abroad over the face of all the earth." (Genesis 11:8-9). Over time, new cultures developed, and changes in the environment produced certain physical traits that became dominant among ethnic groups where there was less intermarrying, creating "a more static set of traits."[156]

This biblical account of the creation and repopulation of the earth tells us that we are all family, God's family. The microscopic details of our DNA connecting us are carefully coded by a kind, loving, and compassionate Creator who longs to see us united in love, peace, and harmony despite differences. Exclusiveness has no place in His family; He forbids it. The Bible offers an example of this unity. In the book of Acts, in St. Paul's sermon on Mars' Hill, his audience consisted of Greek citizens of Athens who felt superior because of their contributions to the performing arts, literature, and culture. Also present were Epicurean and Stoic philosophers who prized their intellect over others. St. Paul admonished his audience: "And He has made from one blood every nation of men to dwell on all the face of the earth, and has determined their pre-appointed times and the boundaries of their dwellings." (Acts 17:26).

His message underscores three essential perspectives:
• The true God of heaven and earth created everything and everyone.

• We are redeemed and unified through His blood.

• There is no preferential treatment in God's eyesight.

Theologian Albert Barnes supported this theme when he said, "All the

---

156 https://www.christianity.com/wiki/Bible/how-did-different-races-come-into-existence-as-gods-wonderful-created-image.html

families of mankind are descended from one origin or stock. However different in their complexion, features, or language, yet they are derived from a common parent."[157]

This position counters the flawed belief that specific ethnic groups are inferior based on genetic traits, race, or ethnicity. Fortunately, human attempts at the same have proven to be failures. We are all loved by God; Jesus died for the entire human race, as revealed in scripture. "For God so loved the world that He gave His only begotten Son, that whoever believes in Him should not perish but have everlasting life." (John 3:16).

Nazi Germany attempted to perpetuate the theory that the Aryan race was the superior race. In 1935, The Nuremberg Laws were passed, the pseudo-scientific basis for racial discrimination. However, when Jessie Owens, an African American, outperformed all other athletes in track and field during the 1936 Olympic Games in Germany, winning four gold medals, the superior race theory became questionable. It gave Hitler fits, as he was using the Olympic Games to showcase Nazi Germany. Bachrach, Susan D. (2000). The Nazi Olympics: Berlin 1936.

Sadly, there is a rise in frightening neo-Nazism. Neo-Nazism denies the occurrence of the Holocaust, recruits neo-Nazi members on social media, and participates in violent protests, such as the "Unite the Right" rally that took place in Charlottesville, Virginia, in August 2017, that was responsible for three deaths.

COLORISM

Another problem facing African Americans is that of "colorism." The National Conference for Community and Justice defines colorism as the "practice of discrimination by which those with lighter skin are treated more favorably than those with darker skin."[158] Colorism is not just a modern problem, either. In biblical times, Moses' siblings' disapproved of his marriage to Zipporah, a woman of color. "Then Miriam and Aaron spoke against Moses because of the Ethiopian woman whom he had married; for he had married an Ethiopian woman." (Numbers 12:1).

In response, God spoke from a cloud over the sanctuary and rebuked Miriam especially, causing her skin to become leprous. Moses pledfor her, and she was forgiven and healed by God after spending seven days outside of the camp.

157 Explanatory and Practical on the Acts of the Apostles Page 262

158 https://www.nccj.org/colorism-0

God's Word expresses His displeasure with discriminatory practices based on color has been established in His Word.

Modern-day colorism continued throughout history, entering the Antebellum South, where slave labor was economically advantageous. Slaves with lighter-skin complexions were selected for work in the plantation owner's home, often because the slaves were the plantation owner's offspring and were less offensive than those with darker skin. Thus, judging people based on skin color creates an oppressive caste system.

Such was the case of President Abraham Lincoln's valet, William Henry Johnson, a freedman who accompanied President Lincoln to the White House in Washington, DC, in 1860. It was an unspoken yet strictly enforced rule that only lighter-skinned slaves would serve in the White House. However, because Johnson had darker skin, he was often mistreated by the White House slaves, who were influenced by the prejudices of the day, until President Lincoln himself intervened.

Even when slavery ended, the preference for European features continued as the bar for acceptable social status among African Americans. Thus, even to the mid-20th century, colorism prevailed in various forms. For instance, the "brown bag" test justifies who receives higher-level employment opportunities, membership in particular churches, and certain African American fraternities and sororities. A few subjects of colorism on the world stage include former President Barack Obama and his wife, Michelle, Meagan, the wife of the Duke of Sussex, and the Vice President of the United States, Kamala Harris.

The issue of colorism seems to be a cycle of warped ideologies. While used as a mechanism during slavery to perpetuate division among African Americans, its roots of practice transcended other cultures as well. This wicked, shameful, yet often unspoken preference for a lighter versus darker skin color, is still prevalent today. Behind the scenes, Satan's work attempts to undermine God's love for humanity, which includes persons of varied hues, even the darkest, who are all precious in His sight.

UNITY IN DIVERSITY REQUIRES UNITY IN CHRIST

The book of Galatians, written by St. Paul from Ephesus around 53-54 CE, amplifies the importance of diversity from a spiritual perspective. His Galatian letter to the churches in the geographical region of Galatia (modern Turkey) strongly promotes the importance of embracing unity in Christ, regardless of racial distinctions. In context, St. Paul wrote this letter due to the rapidly growing

Jewish Messianic movement in Jerusalem, which quickly spread throughout the Roman Empire, promoting Christianity's notion for all humanity.

Remarkably, he discovered during his missionary journeys that there were as many non-Jews as Jews practicing Christianity. This ethnic mix was both a blessing and a challenge for the early Christian Churches in Galatia. At the outset, it was a preview of heaven as people from various ethnic groups assembled weekly for worship and afterward engaged in fellowship potlucks. However, there were Jewish members—gatekeepers in these congregations—who attempted to enforce the observance of the Mosaic Law in the Torah. They wanted to see the law in practice with circumcision and other rituals, which sparked huge debates that threatened the survival of the newly formed Christian churches. In Acts of the Apostles chapter 15, the Council of Jerusalem was formed in 50 CE to address the ongoing debates. Chaired by James, the brother of Jesus, the Council of Jerusalem decreed that Gentile Christians did not have to adhere to all of the requirements of the Mosaic Law.

St. Paul was keenly aware that these Jewish ceremonies were counterproductive to the growth and development of the church. Therefore, he encouraged the believers to embrace and conceptualize Jesus' words in Matthew 5:17 that He had not come to destroy the Law or the Prophets but to fulfill them. They needed to understand that hope must be placed in Jesus' life, death, and resurrection and that even when we demonstrate our best behavior by obeying the law, we still fall short of God's grace. St. Paul further emphasized this point in Ephesians 2:8-9 when he wrote, "For by grace you have been saved through faith, and that not of yourselves; it is the gift of God, not of works, lest anyone should boast."

His message in Galatians is as relevant today as it was in the first century: Galatians 3:28-29 supports this position, stating, "There is neither Jew nor Greek, there is neither slave nor free, there is neither male nor female; for you are all one in Christ Jesus. And if you are in Christ, then you are Abraham's seed and heirs according to the promise." There are no distinctions or boundaries in God's love for His people. In God's eyesight, privilege is not conferred based on the premise of colorism, culture, or country of origin but rather on His matchless love for humanity.

It is not by chance that the Christian Church includes multiple ethnic groups who differ by cultural traditions, physical appearances, socio-economic statuses, and more. Diversification ideally unites us with a shared Christian worldview, values, and supreme love for God and others. Christianity, which embodies the Christian faith, centers on beliefs related to the birth, life, death, and resurrection of Jesus Christ, the ultimate source of unity. Beyond its name, it comes with moral obligations and responsibilities to demonstrate the love of God through practical measures that should include, but not be limited to, authentic "inclusion and integration." Such a demonstration will require overcoming negative racial and ethnic stereotypes that influence attitudes toward others who may be different from oneself.

Americans, daily thriving in an ever-growing melting pot, have been afforded a remarkable opportunity to contribute to a more unified society. What makes America great, along with its beautifully diverse landscape, is the diversity in its cultures, music, foods, religions, etc. God has immensely blessed America, and it is imperative for the survival and sustainability of future generations that the importance of valuing others is learned and made practical in everyday life. America's rich diversity is one of its greatest assets!

The Bible has its share of examples that help clarify unity in diversity. For instance, regarding marriage, the Bible states in Genesis 2:24, "And they shall become one flesh." On the wedding day, a couple enters into a covenant relationship to achieve their life goals. Symbolically, they become one during the wedding ceremony. However, integrating two lives with different backgrounds, i.e., environmental and cultural,, will require much more work that extends far beyond the wedding vows. Yet, many married couples provide irrefutable evidence of unity despite differences, and because they are intentional about becoming one.

The Bible also speaks of the body in 1 Corinthians 12:12, stating that one body consists of many parts, representing multiple functions. "For as the body is one and has many members, but all the members of that one body, being many, are one body, so also is Christ." In context, St. Paul draws an extensive analogy between the human body and the church as a body of believers. Sadly, he needed to address superiority attitudes and some moral issues in the one place where such dispositions should not have existed. Rival factions promulgated to divide the congregation at Corinth. His analogy shows that the body and the church function similarly with different parts and members, but all are essential for optimal functionality and even existence in some cases.

The third example is the Trinity—The Father, Son, and Holy Spirit—which reveals the highest level of diversity with the Godhead's eternal unity and unique functionality. The concept of a Triune God is a widely accepted belief in the

Christian faith that there is one God in three Persons: God the Father, God the Son, and God the Holy Spirit. Although one God, each person of the Godhead is distinct, as the Bible records at Jesus' baptism in Matthew 3:16-17: "When He had been baptized, Jesus came up immediately from the water; and behold, the heavens were opened to Him, and He saw the Spirit of God descending like a dove and alighting upon Him. And suddenly, a voice came from heaven, saying, "This is My beloved Son, in whom I am well pleased." Here the entire Godhead was present, and each carried out a different role.

In John 17:21, Jesus prayed for the unity referenced in these passages because He knew it would be essential to carry out the most important work on earth: The gospel commission— "Go therefore and make disciples of all the nations, baptizing them in the name of the Father and of the Son and of the Holy Spirit." (Matthew 28:19).

In preparation to enter God's kingdom, where all will stand together in an innumerable multitude "of all nations, tribes, peoples, and tongues" (Revelation 7:9), there must be a commitment to unity through God's almighty power. Such a commitment, as well as the thrilling sight of an innumerable multitude, reveals the fulfillment of Isaiah's extraordinary vision: "… Nation shall not lift up sword against nation, neither shall they learn war anymore" (Isaiah 2:4).

REFLECTING MORE ON THE TOPIC:

What were your most meaningful takeaways from this chapter?

____

____

____

____

What will you do differently because of your increased awareness?

____

____

____

____

What resources or support do you need to ensure the successful achievement of your goals?

____

____

____

____

CHAPTER 8

WHERE DO WE GO FROM HERE?

We explored multiple aspects of social justice that were examined from historical, civil and religious perspectives in the previous chapters. A presentation of the issues is a fitting start to understanding the problem, but it does not solve it. So, where do we go from here? Individually and collectively, that is the all-important question to now answer. An examination of issues only is an insufficient response to the colossal problem of social injustice. If the world is to become a better place for all people, action is needed. Reconciliation, dialogue on critical issues, and love can potentially illuminate the path to justice and equality.

CULTURAL COMPETENCE

21st-century technology has made our world smaller and amplified the importance of understanding cultural competence, simply defined as "the ability to work effectively with people from different cultural backgrounds."[159]

Social media, job migration and demographic shifts daily require people from different cultures to interact in the workplace and beyond, ideally to develop professional and meaningful relationships. Without an understanding and appreciation of cultural competence, we are at risk of experiencing a perpetual cultural shock.

There are varied components of cultural competence, including a willingness and desire to understand self and interact and learn about other cultures, religions, and respective worldviews. Cultural competence, at its best, embodies the essence of cultural awareness, which contributes immensely to cultural sensitivity, i.e., greetings, eye contact and personal space. Notably, cultural awareness is key to properly interpreting verbal and non-verbal messages that enable one to make an appropriate relational assessment without being critical.

According to the Pew Research Center, "China has the world's largest pop-

---

159 https://www.globalcognition.org/cultural-competence/

ulation (1.426 billion), but India (1.417 billion) is expected to claim this title next year." As of July 21, 2022, The United States has the third highest population, with "338 million."[160]

Interesting to note is that "more than 40 million people living in the U.S. were born in another country, accounting for about one-fifth of the world's migrants."[161]

The importance of cultural competence is appropriately substantiated by the large migrant population in the United States, which is metaphorically referred to as a melting pot due to its expansive multi-ethnic population. However, during former President Donald Trump's administration, the nation experienced a historic decrease in legal immigrants, making him "Successful in reducing legal immigration."[162]

Perhaps, limited consideration was given to the notion that legal immigrants make a positive impact on the economy as they increase the labor force and the potential number of entrepreneurs and taxpayers. Beyond these obvious reasons, faith groups should encourage educating and practicing what is written in the Torah and scriptures regarding immigrants, noting that we use many terms today for what the Bible calls strangers, foreigners, and sojourners, i.e., immigrants, migrants, displaced persons, refugees, and asylum seekers.

These references make it clear that God's view on treating migrants with compassion, dignity, and respect has no expiration date. The story of slavery in America is a story of resilient people who arrived not as immigrants or indentured servants but people who were forced into harsh labor, and God liberated them through His miraculous power. Their difficult journey has influenced cultural sensitivity that everyone, regardless of where they were born, has a story and is valued.

WE ARE NOT TO OPPRESS IMMIGRANTS.

"Also, you shall not oppress a stranger, for you know the heart of a stranger because you were strangers in the land of Egypt." Exodus 23:9

"And if a stranger dwells with you in your land, you shall not mistreat him. The stranger who dwells among you shall be to you as one born among you, and you shall love him as yourself; for you were strangers in the land of Egypt: I am

---

160 https://worldpopulationreview.com/countries/united-states-population

161 https://www.pewresearch.org/fact-tank/2020/08/20/key-findings-about-u-s-immigrants/

162 https://www.cato.org/blog/president-trump-reduced-legal-immigration-he-did-not-reduce-illegal-immigration

the Lord your God." Leviticus 19:33-34.

"He administers justice for the fatherless and the widow and loves the stranger, giving him food and clothing. Therefore love the stranger, for you were strangers in the land of Egypt." (Deuteronomy 10:18-19).

WE SHOULD SHOW JUSTICE TO FOREIGNERS

"Do not take advantage of a hired worker who is poor and needy, whether that worker is a fellow Israelite or a foreigner residing in one of your towns. Pay them their wages each day before sunset because they are poor and are counting on it. Otherwise, they may cry to the Lord against you, and you will be guilty of sin." (Deuteronomy 24:14-15).

"And I will come near you for judgment; I will be a swift witness Against sorcerers, Against adulterers, Against perjurers, Against those who exploit wage earners and widows and orphans, And against those who turn away an alien— Because they do not fear Me," Says the Lord of hosts." (Malachi 3:5).

"Thus says the Lord: "Execute judgment and righteousness, and deliver the plundered out of the hand of the oppressor. Do no wrong and do no violence to the stranger, the fatherless, or the widow, nor shed innocent blood in this place." (Jeremiah 23:3).

"It shall be that you will divide it by lot as an inheritance for yourselves and for the strangers who dwell among you and who bear children among you. They shall be to you as native-born among the children of Israel; they shall have an inheritance with you among the tribes of Israel. And it shall be that in whatever tribe the stranger dwells, there you shall give him his inheritance," says the Lord God." (Ezekiel 47:22-23).

Thus says the Lord of hosts: "Execute true justice, show mercy and compassion, Everyone to his brother. Do not oppress the widow or the fatherless, the alien or the poor. Let none of you plan evil in his heart against his brother." (Zechariah 7:9-10).

RECONCILIATION

Reconciliation is highly relational, described as the process of seeking forgiveness for past wrongs and "the full acceptance of our collective biography and its consequences."[163] It is further based on the premise that there has been a breakdown in a relationship, and it inherently involves change that results in

---

163 Ta-Nehisi Coates, 10."The Case for Reparations," *The Atlantic*, June 2014

harmony and relationship restoration.

America has some reconciliatory work to do. The mighty nation that proclaims "In God We Trust" is encouraged to acknowledge and seek forgiveness for past wrongs, with slavery being among its most prominent debasements. Reconciliation is not easy, but possible. The counsel of Joshua, Moses' successor, would be a good start. In his farewell speech to Israel (Joshua 23), Joshua challenged Israel to remain faithful to God because they would be incapable in their own strength. Likewise, God's power is essential for genuine reconciliation to occur. Reconciliation includes acknowledging that the slave labor in America that required slaves to work from sunrise to sunset was crucial to capitalism but was inhumane, immoral, and wrong.

Much of the wealth from slave labor came from the southern states, which produced most of the cotton shipped to England. During The Industrial Revolution, the invention of the mechanical cotton gin by Eli Whitney in 1793 created many millionaires. Mississippi, the nation's largest cotton-producing state, was financially and politically dependent on cotton, as were many other southern states. By 1860, so much wealth was in Mississippi from cotton that it became one of the wealthiest states in the entire country. Slaves and slave labor were considered highly valued commodities. During this same period, "over $3 billion was the value assigned to the physical bodies of enslaved Black Americans to be used as free labor and production." [164]

While the signing of the Emancipation Proclamation freed over four million slaves, they received no compensation or benefits. The former slaves were unprepared but expected to survive their new freedom without a blueprint. James Weldon Johnson described the journey from slavery to freedom; and wrote the Negro National Anthem "Stony the road we trod, Bitter the chastening rod, Felt in the days when hope unborn had died." How different might their lot have been had they followed the biblical narrative, where the Egyptians cooperated with God before freeing the Israelites: "And the Lord had given the people favor in the sight of the Egyptians, so that they granted them what they requested." (Exodus 12:36).

Despite the bleak views and perceptions of slow progress, the path toward reconciliation can shine brighter with every step taken in the right direction. The ideal state requires embracing the principles of God's kingdom, which include equality and justice for all. It is the glorious kingdom that the Prophet Isaiah

---

[164] https://www.brookings.edu/policy2020/bigideas/why-we-need-reparations-for-black-americans/

anticipated when he penned the words, "He shall judge between the nations, And rebuke many people; They shall beat their swords into plowshares, and their spears into pruning hooks; Nation shall not lift up sword against nation, neither shall they learn war anymore." (Isaiah 2:4). The sculptor Evgeniy Vuchetich (1908-1974) depicts Isaiah's vision of the glorious future with an impressive sculpture in the United Nations Garden which reads: "Let Us Beat Swords into Plowshares."

THE CROSS OF CHRIST RECONCILES

The cross of Christ represents the pivotal point of reconciliation between God and humanity, a theme central to Christian theology. It is imperative that the Christian community embrace the death of Christ on the cross as a key step in reconciliation as He died for humanity.

In obedience, Christ, our High Priest offered Himself as a "propitiatory sacrifice" for our sins on the cross (Hebrews 2:5–18, Hebrews 5:1–10; Romans. 3:21–26). The Greek word "katallage," used by St. Paul in Romans 5:10–11, 2 Corinthians 5:18–21, Ephesians 2:11–22, and Colossians 1:19–20 when translated, means reconciliation thorough change, or transformation. The sacrificial act of Christ serves as an immense demonstration of divine love and mercy, resolving the conflict brought about by human sinfulness. Through the crucifixion, Jesus took upon himself the rightful punishment for humanity's transgressions, thereby satisfying the demands of divine justice. As a result, the way is opened for humanity to be reconciled with God.

The death of Christ on the cross was "to restore, to bring together, or make peace between two estranged or hostile parties. It also brought together those once opposed to each other based on barriers set by culture, class and religion, such as the struggle experienced in the 1st Century Church between Jews and Gentiles (Romans 11:25, 17-18; Ephesians 2:11-12). However, scripture also reminds us that Jesus Christ is the agent of peace who has broken down the dividing wall between Jews and Gentiles (Ephesians 2:13-15). Through the death of Christ on the cross, Jesus fulfilled the requirements of the law and reconciled both Jews and Gentiles to God. The result is a new humanity, a united body of believers, in which all can approach God as one, by the indwelling of the Holy Spirit. Fortunately, the Gentiles became fellow believers with their Jewish counterparts, forming one body and one temple with Christ as the Cornerstone. Christ reconciles us vertically to God by bearing our sin (Romans 5:1–2; Ephesians 2:17–18, 3:12, Hebrews. 10:19–22), and horizontally with one another, including those who may feel alienated.

Clearly, unity among believers is essential within the realm of Christianity and is amplified accordingly throughout the Bible. Now is the time to respond to the clarion call to authentically embrace and model reconciliation through the common faith we have been afforded in Jesus Christ, the One through whom all believers are reconciled to God. May we all seize the magnanimous power of the Cross to ignite a much-needed transformation that will reconcile us to both God and humanity. Unity is sure to follow.

THE STATUE OF LIBERTY

The Statue of Liberty, an iconic copper statue in the New York Harbor, was proposed by "Edouard de Laboulaye, the French political thinker, U.S. Constitution expert, and abolitionist" and dedicated in 1886.[165]

The right hand of the Statue of Liberty holds a torch above her head, and the left hand a tablet with the date of the Declaration of Independence inscribed in Roman numerals. "The Statue of Liberty was a symbol of democratic government and Enlightenment ideals, as well as a celebration of the Union's victory in the American Civil War and the abolition of slavery."[166]

The broken shackle and chain on her feet "Was not yet a reality for African Americans."

On the other hand, to European immigrants arriving at Ellis Island, the Statue of Liberty symbolized hope and opportunity.

In his autobiography, W.E.B. Du Bois, an African American sociologist, historian, and civil rights activist, recalled seeing the Statue of Liberty on a return trip from Europe in 1894. Many immigrants were excited about coming to America. "But he didn't talk to any of them. The ship was segregated." (*Washington Post*, May 23, 2019). "Instead of representing freedom and justice for all, the Statue of Liberty emphasized the bitter ironies of America's professed identity as a just and free society for all people, regardless of race."[167]

Sadly, this great symbol of freedom and liberty resides in a divided nation where African Americans, in particular, seem to be victimized among those denied true liberty, justice, and equality.

Among these is "privilege," defined by Merriam-Webster's dictionary "as

---

165 https://www.nps.gov/stli/learn/historyculture/abolition.htm

166 https://www.nps.gov/stli/learn/historyculture/abolition.htm

167 Ibid.

a right or immunity granted as a peculiar benefit, advantage, or favor." Most often, privilege in America has been afforded to White Non-Hispanic Ethnic Groups. "White privilege is the automatic, taken-for-granted advantage bestowed upon white people as a result of living in a society based on the premise of white as the human ideal."[168]

White privilege is viewed as a sense of entitlement due to skin color, with Whites determining who can be considered white. "White privilege denotes both obvious and less obvious passive advantages that white people may not recognize they have, which distinguishes it from overt bias or prejudice."[169]

White privilege was most visible during the Jim Crow era in the following ways: public transportation, restaurants, restrooms, theaters, water fountains, and municipal swimming pools. In southern states, African Americans stepped to the side when a white person approached them on the streets and drove behind white enforcement officers to avoid receiving a traffic ticket. When African Americans went to court in Georgia, they "were sworn in with separate Bibles."[170]

The social justice-conscious of America cannot repudiate the appalling history of slavery for over 400 years. While the present generation is not responsible for the merciless servitude of slavery, they nevertheless inherited economic, academic, and political advantages from those who did, which has contributed significantly to their success. Jesus said, "For everyone to whom much is given, from him much will be required; and to whom much has been committed, of him, they will ask the more." (Luke 12:48). Those capable of making charitable gifts and establishing endowments, educational scholarships to improve the lives of the disadvantaged over the centuries should do so because with privilege comes responsibility.

Reparations could reasonably address some of the inequities that have rippled over generations of African Americans. Other ethnic groups have received reparations for disparate treatment: Native Americans, Japanese Americans, and Holocaust survivors. The possibility of descendants of former slaves receiving reparations from the United States federal government is part of an intense discussion in the nation. A reparations bill was first proposed in 1989 by the late United States Representative John Conyers, Jr.(D), Michigan's 1st Congressio-

---

168 https://www.cbsnews.com/news/white-privilege-racism-ibram-x-kendi-robin-diangelo/

169 https://en.wikipedia.org/wiki/White_privilege

170 https://www.georgiaencyclopedia.org/articles/history-archaeology/segregation

nal District, with the purpose of creating a commission to study and submit a formal report to Congress and the American people. The bill was reintroduced on January 4, 2021, by United States Representative Shelia Jackson Lee (D), Texas' 18th Congressional District. United States Senator Cory Booker (D) of New Jersey is the sponsor of a companion bill in the Senate. Until the subject of reparations is resolved, African Americans should continue modeling examples of faith, education, and economic empowerment for subsequent generations.

RESTITUTION IS BIBLICAL

Reparations or compensation is biblical and should be performed by the guilty party. Restitution does exist in the Old and New Testaments. Reparations should include three elements according to the late William Darity an American economist and social sciences researcher at Duke University " (a) acknowledgement of the wrongs done, (b) payment for the wrongs done, and (c) closure for both parties." https://www.thegospelcoalition.org/blogs/thabiti-anyabwile/reparations-are-biblical/

Whoever steals an ox or a sheep and slaughters it or sells it must pay back five head of cattle for the ox and four sheep for the sheep. Exodus 22:1

"If the stolen animal is found alive in their possession—whether ox or donkey or sheep—they must pay back double." Exodus 22:4

"If anyone gives a neighbor silver or goods for safekeeping and they are stolen from the neighbor's house, the thief, if caught, must pay back double." Exodus 22:7

"Maintaining love to thousands, and forgiving wickedness, rebellion and sin. Yet he does not leave the guilty unpunished; he punishes the children and their children for the sin of the parents to the third and fourth generation." Exodus 34:7

"Then it shall be, because he has sinned and is guilty, that he shall restore what he has stolen, or the thing which he has extorted, or what was delivered to him for safekeeping, or the lost thing which he found, or all that about which he has sworn falsely. He shall restore its full value, add one-fifth more to it, and give it to whomever it belongs, on the day of his trespass offering." Leviticus 6:4-5

"If your brother, a Hebrew man, or a Hebrew woman, is sold to you and serves you six years, then in the seventh year you shall let him go free from you. And when you [a]send him away free from you, you shall not let him go away empty-handed; you shall supply him liberally from your flock, from your thresh-ing floor, and from your winepress. From what the Lord your God has blessed you with, you shall give to him. You shall remember that you were a slave in the land of Egypt, and the Lord your God redeemed you; therefore I command you this thing today." Deuteronomy 15:12-15

"Yet you say, 'Why should the son not bear the guilt of the father?' Because the son has done what is lawful and right, and has kept all My statutes and observed them, he shall surely live. The soul who sins shall die. The son shall not bear the guilt of the father, nor the father bear the guilt of the son. The righ-teousness of the righteous shall be upon himself, wand the wickedness of the wicked shall be upon himself. Ezekiel 18:19–20

"Then Zacchaeus stood and said to the Lord, "Look, Lord, I give half of my goods to the poor; and if I have taken anything from anyone by false accusation, I restore fourfold." Luke 19:8

LOVE WILL CONQUER ALL

The inspiring words of Dr. Martin Luther Kings, Jr.: "Darkness cannot drive out darkness; only light can do that. Hate cannot drive out hate; only love can do that" suggest love will conquer all, including what appears foreign to human nature. Love is the motivating force in the lives of men and women to embrace each other without fear, evil intent, or malice. When we commit ourselves to love and not hate, we follow the command of Jesus to His disciples. In John 13:34-35, Jesus said, "A new command I give you: Love one another. As I have loved you, so you must love one another. By this, everyone will know that you are my disciples if you love one another."

This command inherently includes our enemies because returning hate for hate multiplies hate, increasing the darkness of the night.

During a trip to Rwanda, I became more aware of the positive effects that love can have over hate. The Rwandan genocide took place from April 7 - July 15, 1994, between the Tutsi and Hutu. An estimated 800,000 Rwandans were killed in the space of 100 days."[171]

One of many stories that captured my attention was of a man and his wife who narrowly escaped death. Some of their family members were killed and bur-ied in mass graves, leaving children without parents and, in some cases, home-

---

[171] Rwanda: How the genocide happened Archived 22 October 2018 at the Wayback Machine, BBC, 17 May 2011

less. They explained that some of the perpetrators were once respected church members, community leaders, and family members. This couple was from different tribes and determined, with God's help, that they would demonstrate, through authentic forgiveness, that love is more vital than tribalism.

The life story of the late Holocaust survivor Eva Mozes Kor represents true forgiveness on every level. Eva and her twin sister Miriam were subjected to human experimentation under SS Doctor Josef Mengele at the Auschwitz concentration camp.

Eva's parents and two older sisters died in the gas chambers at Birkenau; only she and Miriam survived. After the end of World War II, she immigrated to Israel and later to the United States. In 1984, Eva founded CANDLES (Children of Auschwitz Nazi Deadly Lab Experiments Survivors). Eva demonstrated the spirit of forgiveness when in the 1990s, she took a bold step forward and forgave all the Nazis, including Mengele and Adolf Hitler.

She even traveled to Germany in 2015 to testify in the trial of former Nazi Oskar Gröning. During the trial, she and Gröning shared an embrace. Eva thanked Gröning for testifying to what happened more than seventy years earlier. One of my favorite quotes from her is, "Forgiveness is a seed for peace. It is the ultimate act of self-healing." Until we seek to forgive and move forward, the past will imprison us.

The late congressman John Lewis said, "When you see something that is not right, not fair, not just, you have to speak up. You have to say something; you have to do something."

Others should not feel comfortable making offensive remarks in the workplace, church, or school, but rather be respectfully corrected with patience, as well as a heart of forgiveness. Injustices, inequality, racism, discrimination, and prejudice often seem perpetual and enduring, requiring forgiveness at a proportionate level.

Jesus amplified the critical role of forgiveness in The Lord's Prayer when He said, "And forgive us our debts, As we forgive our debtors." (Matthew 6:12). The message in this scriptural text seems to be that God will forgive us based on our willingness to forgive others. And while the Bible further states, "He that covereth his sins shall not prosper: but whoso confesseth and forsaketh them shall have mercy" Proverbs 28:13, our forgiveness of others is not conditional upon their confession or remorsefulness of the wrong action. Forgiveness comes with many benefits, as reported by the Mayo Clinic.[172] Aside from improved health and peace of mind, forgiveness can lead to:

- Healthier relationships

- Improved mental health

- Less anxiety, stress, and hostility

- Lower blood pressure

- Fewer symptoms of depression

- A stronger immune system

- Improved heart health

- Improved self-esteem

Though complex in practice, Jesus' admonition to Peter is relevant. When Peter asked Jesus, "Lord, how often shall my brother sin against me, and I forgive him? Up to seven times?" Jesus said to him, "I do not say to you, up to seven times, but up to seventy times seven." (Matthew 18:21-22). Jesus is saying, do not count the number of times you extend forgiveness, but do it continually, treating the offense as if it never occurred. It is clearly His love that can make any semblance of this occurring. For love, God's love, conquers all.

In I Corinthians 13, St. Paul accentuated the importance of nonnegotiable love and acceptance of one another. "Love suffers long and is kind; love does not envy; love does not parade itself, is not puffed up; does not behave rudely, does not seek its own, is not provoked, thinks no evil; does not rejoice in iniquity, but rejoices in the truth; bears all things, believes all things, hopes all things, endures all things." (I Corinthians 13:4-7). This type of love is authentic with the capacity to extinguish the fire of segregation and can go much deeper than a mission trip, volunteering in a food pantry, or providing financial support. It highlights the love that Christ taught:

"This is My commandment, that you love one another as I have loved you. Greater love has no one than this, than to lay down one's life for his friends." (John 15:12-13).

"But I say to you, love your enemies, bless those who curse you, do good to those who hate you, and pray for those who spitefully use you and persecute

---

172 https://www.mayoclinic.org/healthy-lifestyle/adult-health/in-depth/forgiveness/art-20047692

you, that you may be sons of your Father in heaven; for He makes His sun rise on the evil and on the good, and sends rain on the just and on the unjust." (Matthew 5:44-45).

"Beloved, let us love one another, for love is of God; and everyone who loves is born of God and knows God. He who does not love does not know God, for God is love." (1 John 4:7-8).

"And be kind to one another, tenderhearted, forgiving one another, even as God in Christ forgave you." (Ephesians 4:32).

We are waiting in the doorway passage of our earthbound world for Jesus to proclaim that His intercessory work is completed in the heavenly sanctuary, and and for His victorious return as a conquering King. The conflict of the ages between Christ and Satan will soon be over, and Satan, the evil angels, the unrighteous, and death will be eternally defeated. The Bible tells us that "Affliction will not rise a second time." (Nahum 1:9). On judgement day, everyone will be held accountable for both their good and bad deeds. That is why it is imperative that we act on the principle of what honors God and not what is socially, politically, and culturally acceptable. For it is written: "As I live, says the Lord, Every knee shall bow to Me, And every tongue shall confess to God." So then each of us shall give an account of himself to God." (Romans 14:11-12).

Afterwards, the multi-ethnic family of God will declare throughout the universe that God is love. John the Revelator wrote of this reunion: "After these things I looked, and behold, a great multitude which no one could number, of all nations, tribes, peoples, and tongues, standing before the throne and before the Lamb, clothed with white robes, with palm branches in their hands." (Revelation 7:9). In heaven, the redeemed will eat from the tree of life in God's kingdom whose leaves are for the healing of the nations." (Revelation 22:2). The reference to the leaves of that tree being for the "healing of the nations" means God will remove all ethnic barriers. He will restore all people, tribes, and nations into one harmonious family, living in perfect peace for eternity.

NEVER GIVE UP–THE FUTURE IS BRIGHT

Jewish tradition recounts a story of a rabbi who, looking into the sleepy eyes of the young men in his classroom, asked: "Students, when does one know when the night is ended and the day has begun?" Several of the students cautiously raised their hands. "Rabbi," one asked, "is it when you can tell the difference between a fig tree and an olive tree?"

"No."

Another student raised his hand: "Rabbi, is it when you can tell the difference between a sheep and a goat?"

After listening to a host of answers, the rabbi announced, "Students, one knows the night has ended, and the day has begun when you can look at a face never before seen and recognize the stranger as a brother or sister. Until that moment, no matter how bright the day, it is still the night."

It may be night still, but we can never give up on the hope of a bright future. As long as there is God, whose existence is eternal, there is hope.

In 2019, the Pew Research Center reported that "a majority of Americans say race relations in the United States are bad, and of those, about seven in ten say things are getting even worse." In 2020, the Pew Research Center reported, "Most Americans see a recent increased focus on issues of race as a turning point; about half say it will result in policy and societal changes." Though a colossal issue, rays of hope illuminate with every concerted act toward freedom, justice, and equality. Robert Kennedy's words eloquently speak to the same: "Each time a man stands up for an ideal or acts to improve a lot of others, or strikes out against injustice, he sends forth a tiny ripple of hope, and crossing each other from a million different centers of energy and daring, those ripples build a current that can sweep down the mightiest walls of oppression and resistance." Robert F. Kennedy, University of Capetown, June 6, 1966.

The time has come to courageously stand on the right side of social justice and take seriously the words of the ancient prophet, Isaiah: "Cry aloud, spare not; Lift up your voice like a trumpet; Tell My people their transgression, And the house of Jacob their sins." Isaiah 58:1 Both clergy and laity are challenged to use the sacred desk to address the significance of social justice, making it an integral part of the lectionary calendar.

Hopeful hearts must also proclaim the approaching Year of Jubilee at the second coming of Christ that will bring liberty to all willing to receive it. The word jubilee in the Old Testament is taken from the Hebrew word yobel meaning "a ram's horn, or trumpet." Jubilee was the sabbatical year after seven cycles of seven years (49 years). The fiftieth year was to be a time of celebration and rejoicing for the Israelites. In the book of Leviticus, Hebrew slaves and prisoners would be freed, debts would be forgiven, and the mercies of God would be extended to all people. Leviticus 25:8–13 In the New Testament the jubilee theme is symbolic of Jesus as the liberator who came to set us free from the slavery of sin. His death on the cross settled our sin debt and provided a means for our restoration to God the Father.

"For the wages of sin is death, but the gift of God is eternal life in Christ Jesus our Lord." Romans 3:23

"And having been set free from sin, you became slaves of righteousness." Romans 6:18

"Stand fast therefore in the liberty by which Christ has made us free, and do not be entangled again with a yoke of bondage." Galatians 5:1

When the time of Jubilee comes and Christ returns, we are promised that "Every valley shall be exalted And every mountain and hill brought low; The crooked places shall be made straight And the rough places smooth." Isaiah 40:4 The heavens and the earth await that glorious Jubilee with great excitement when the sands of time shall turn into eternity!

For nearly 7,000 years, the world has been in peril, causing some to anxiously anticipate the second coming of Christ, the planet's only hope for righting all wrongs. The return of Christ is imminent and predicted multiple times in scripture:

"For the Son of Man will come in the glory of His Father with His angels, and then He will reward each according to his works." (Matthew 16:27).

"For as the lightning comes from the east and flashes to the west, so also will the coming of the Son of Man be." (Matthew 24:27).

"Then they will see the Son of Man coming in a cloud with power and great glory." (Luke 21:27).

"And if I go and prepare a place for you, I will come again and receive you to Myself; that where I am, there you may be also." (John 14:3).

"This same Jesus, who was taken up from you into heaven, will so come in like manner as you saw Him go into heaven." (Acts 1:11-12).

"Looking for the blessed hope and glorious appearing of our great God and Savior Jesus Christ." (Titus 2:13).

"And behold, I am coming quickly, and My reward is with Me, to give to every one according to his work." (Revelation 22:12).

Christ is presently interceding in the heavenly sanctuary where he will proclaim one day, "He who is unjust, let him be unjust still; he who is filthy, let him be filthy still; he who is righteous, let him be righteous still; he who is holy, let him be holy still." (Revelation 22:11).

Christ will return to the earth with the holy angels, and the righteous dead will be resurrected, and the righteous living will meet Christ in the air and together, they will receive their reward of eternal life. (1 Thessalonians 4:16-17). The unrighteous living will be slain by God's brightness, and the unrighteous die will remain in their graves until Christ and the righteous return to earth after one-thousand years, called The Millennium. During the one-thousand-year period in heaven, the righteous will reign with Christ and examine the records of heaven that will vindicate the character of Christ against Satan's false claims. (Revelation 20:1-6).

After the conclusion of the one thousand years, Satan and his evil angels and the resurrected unrighteous will receive their verdict and "Every knee shall bow to Me, And every tongue shall confess to God." (Romans 14:11). They will receive their just reward of death by fire that will purify the earth.

Afterwards, God will recreate a new earth which will be the home of the redeemed, and the universe will be liberated from sin. "Affliction will never rise again." (Nahum 1:9). The possibility of sin ever entering the world again is impossible. It will never take place, making way for universal love and acceptance between all people. However, until that day, we must redeem the time by making the most of every opportunity by walking in light and wisdom "See then that you walk circumspectly, not as fools but as wise, redeeming the time…" (Ephesians 5:15-16).

Praise God for the bright and sure future of life, love, liberty, justice, freedom, and equality because of the reality of the soon and imminent return of Jesus Christ!

REFLECTING MORE ON THE TOPIC:

What were your most meaningful takeaways from this chapter?

____

____

____

____

What will you do differently because of your increased awareness?

____

____

____

____

What resources or support do you need to ensure the successful achievement of your goals?

____

____

____

____